THAILAND BOUND
Stories.

Real Tales of Loves
and Losses in
The Land of Smiles

By

Peter Hopkins

THAILAND BOUND STORIES

PETER HOPKINS

Acknowledgements & Contributions

This book contains real stories of Thailand, written and sent over to Peter's YouTube Channel, **'Thailand Bound,'** by his subscribers.

Tales are told through the author's own voice.

Originally edited by Peter Hopkins.

Character names have been changed

Copy edited, formatted, and proofread by Andrew Hammond.

Published May 2022

THAILAND BOUND STORIES

Table of Contents

Story

Page No

Page No

Story 1.

Soul Mate

Some years back my wife and I met a British guy and single father living in the States, who would come out to SE Asia periodically for all the usual reasons. He also wanted to meet up with his 'soul mate' out here. We met him in a small city in Thailand where he told my wife and I, his story.

As with many western men, he had subscribed to the various online Asian dating sites and had connected with one young Thai lovely at some point several years ago. He came out to Thailand, met her and they absolutely clicked and hit it off together. He was slender and good-looking, and the object of his desire was a young Thai in her early twenties. He courted her and they toured together happily to resorts, to Bangkok, and all over. He enjoyed all the pleasures and benefits that a young twenty-something Thai girl might accord him behind closed doors, and he declared outright that he felt like he had met his SOUL MATE.

'Soul Mate' is an interesting term and describes what is depressingly rare in any universe; a situation where two people can just click and get along fabulously, a perfect match for each other. During his month's holiday, he was laughing, dancing, and swimming the beach resorts from Hua Hin to Phuket, which were all great fun. All good things must come to an end, as did his tourist visa.

He had to return to the States where he promised to wrap up his affairs, arrange for his full-time return, then he and she, together with his young daughter would live forever in joy and happiness, presumably with the lovely guy banging his brains out on a consistent basis till he died from exhaustion in his old age. Soul mates!

A week after his return, he's on Facebook... and sees his soul mate's profile and a post showing her current events, in her in a traditional Thai wedding dress, her bloated, bald Australian husband happily embracing her, and our acquaintance's future plans with his soulmate were suddenly, crushed!

It isn't an unusual story at all, and easily replicated in Thailand or other such countries. I often wonder what happened to him. But his tale, along with your own reported stories about bar girls' greed (not to say that EVERY Thai woman is some sort of gold-digger), are great cautionary stories. I have one other friend who is 'happily married' to a Thai girl who is certainly young enough and sexy enough, but still he has a massage woman who is married with four kids, who constantly lets him know that her husband is a typical Thai unfaithful type, with whom she hasn't made love with for years and hints strongly that she would happily provide 'full service' to him would he be interested. He's a pretty 'straight' guy and the notion of hooking up with her is somewhat unappealing to him, but well... he's only tempted, but not really ever going to act on it.

For me, I'm sixty-eight years old and relatively happily married to my Filipina wife of nearly forty years and the relationship isn't perfect because neither of us are 'perfect.' But well... life goes on. Thanks for your stories and cautionary considerations.

Story 2.

Reviewing the Situation

Hi Peter, I follow your channel and was glad to see that you made it back to Thailand this year (2022). I have also made it back, spending thirty days in Phuket.

I am an older Australian guy, now sixty-seven. I have spent a lot of time in Thailand over the years. No plans to live there because I do become jaded at times, mainly with other farang antics. I write this after listening to a story about four men of a certain ethnic background who attacked a girl in Pattaya. I'm sure you know the story I refer too. Back in 2018 I was in BKK and having a few beers with a Thai girl I knew well; she was around forty years old and very pretty. I was a regular customer, she worked in a very popular bar in Soi 4. We headed back to my hotel, a well-known hotel and part of a worldwide chain. We entered the lift and the doors closed then reopened. Three large men of that same ethnic background tried to get into the lift, I raised my hand for them to stop but they pushed into the small lift. The girl huddled behind me; she was very street wise. They started straight away obviously mildly intoxicated and full of bravado.

Comments like, 'you boom boom her, send her to our room next,' etc. etc.

I told them to stop!

One tried to grab at her and I pushed him back with both hands to the chest. I am reasonably fit and worked in the emergency services back home. I am also a quiet guy but not backward in coming forward. The lift doors opened at our floor, I put the girl out and proceeded to ask them to come out of the lift as I had, had enough of them. They declined, instead opting to remain in the lift.

I put the girl in the room and went to the main desk to report their behaviour. No one was interested and as such,

I said, "If it was one of your staff alone in the lift, they may have been assaulted.

Still not much interest.

The next morning at breakfast, the three were sitting eating, I challenged them for causing a small scene. I went and had a meeting with the day manager stating I wanted them out of the hotel. I got no joy from that so told them I would check out and wanted a refund of two days. They did this OK probably just to get rid of me. Funnily enough, I have never done a bad review of any establishment but did one on this hotel's response.

A few hours later I received an email from the hotel chain apologizing and offering two days accommodation at any of their hotels, free. The condition was, that I delete the review. I didn't delete it and replied no thanks. I am sure this type of behavior is in all types, but I have to say I have shared lifts many times with intoxicated men and never had a problem.

****

Story 3.

M for Madness

I became fascinated with Thailand while stopping over in Bangkok airport. I was on my way to Taiwan to visit the parents of my future wife. Long story short, I didn't marry my Taiwanese girlfriend because it just didn't feel right at the time. She is very happy now and I have no regrets with the decision. Part of the reason was, on my brief visit to Bangkok airport, I had felt the charm of the Thai people. The warm welcoming smile and the way they greeted you. Thai people smile so much that it makes you want to constantly smile back.

From that one stopover, I decided to convince my friends and visit Thailand, visiting Bangkok and Phuket in 2012. It was very strange landing in Bangkok for the first time. Being from England, I couldn't figure out why everything was so cheap. I then realised that things aren't cheap in Asia, things are just overpriced in England.

Jet-lagged and confused about what to do, I then smelled the famous Thai dish, Pad Thai on the street. I saw an elderly man using a wok while his wife would prepare the fresh ingredients. I decided to try this authentic street food. After handing over my Thai Baht, I realised that I've just spent 50p for something that gave me a full stomach.

I was alone, as my friends were arriving the next morning in Phuket, so I had a night of wandering from bar to bar. The next morning, I had booked a VIP car from Bangkok to Phuket. The car wasn't quite VIP, it was just a mini-bus full of strangers. There was a Swedish girl, two chilled out Dutch guys, two young skating type rebellious Western guys, who would call each other dudes, and a middle aged, over opinionated angry Western guy with his Thai wife.

A car full of eight strangers, all expecting a VIP experience, only to be crammed into a ten-year-old Toyota people carrier with stale air con, so it came as no surprise that we were all disappointed and the angry Western guy had expressed himself to the driver by asking where was his VIP car? The

Thai driver didn't seem to understand him, staying calm, he kept a poker face only for the angry Western guy to shout even louder. Like the Thai driver would magically understand English because he was now raising his voice.

"Oh yeah, here's your private VIP car sir, I understand English now, I didn't before because you were talking at a normal level."

So doing the English gentleman thing, I decided to calm the angry Western guy down by explaining that we were all in the same boat, or in this case 'Mini-bus.'

The journey was to last for twelve hours and although very cramped, my karma was being instantly rewarded that day as I was squashed up next to the Swedish girl. Everything about her was very Swedish. The blonde hair, accent and her openness to towards rubbing body parts next to strangers. She was the kind of Swedish girl who would enter a sauna naked after she danced naked on the beach at 3am during their hundred days of sunshine in Sweden. To add to my journey, I was seated next to two fun loving Dutch guys who were a joke a minute. Between the four of us we managed to calm the angry Western guy down.

He went from 'I want to knock this Thai man's block off' to 'I'll just sit quietly in the rear back seat'.

The twelve hours didn't seem like twelve hours because we were constantly making jokes about everything that goes wrong in Thailand. How a VIP car is not really a VIP experience and how you can find a McDonalds fast food restaurant in a hospital. I quickly learned that showing the soles of your feet in public to Thai people is considered very rude but shooting ping pong balls from one's private parts is fine. I've always been a very serious person, but Thailand really changed my outlook on life. How we can choose to be angry towards a situation like the angry Western guy or we can choose to just see the funny side to things like the two Dutch guys did. Not only did I have the most amazing road trip of laughter, I woke up in Phuket with the sweaty head of a Swedish blonde on my shoulder. We later exchanged details and YouTube will not approve of what happened next.

My first memory of Phuket was visiting the bars at nighttime. There was a bar called the Freedom bar, owned by a British guy who served time in HM prison. Hence the name of the bar after he served his time. It was a strange feeling walking into a bar and being greeted by so many girls. Although it wasn't a bar where you can take the girls home, all the staff were so welcoming. The owner then gave us a guide on what to do and what bars to visit. The next bar we visited; we were jumped on by the girls. We were all very strong guys and the girls jumped on us and started making funny sexual noises that resembled a squeaking bed.

We were laughing so hard that I struggled to stand up straight. I almost fell to the floor and had to use the bar top to support myself. A girl jumped off me and she jumped onto my not so strong friend and they both ended up on the floor. I laughed so hard that I nearly wet myself. The night went on and at one point I needed to use the toilet. Stumbling to the toilets, I was amazed at the ice filled urinals and it was oddly satisfying melting them with my beer fueled pee. And then to my horror, my neck snapped. Twice and then a little Thai man put me into a headlock. Something that Macho Man Randy Savage would do to Hulk Hogan during Wrestle Mania. My hands being tied up, I had no control over where to point my dick. He would then crack my back and as he did so, a pee would go to the next urinal. After I finished peeing, I left a 100 Baht tip for that very Thai experience. On reflection, no guide in the world can prepare you for this.

"Beware of men snapping your neck in the toilets and asking for your money," said no part of the Lonely Planet book ever.

The next time I needed to pee, I would wait for someone to go before me so that he was busy. But what a unique Thai experience. On meeting my first bar girl, I fell head over heels with a girl called M. She was so beautiful and had the smiles of a thousand super models. If her aunty was a celebrity, it would be Lucy Lui in her prime. M had beautiful cheekbones, a slim body with golden brown skin. Her eyes just glowed, and her lips just spelt 'take my money now!'

This seemed too good to be true to be able to take this gorgeous girl away by paying for a guy drink and bar fine. She sat on the back of my scooter and hugged me while the wind went through our hair. We took a midnight walk along the beach with the moonlight guiding us. We relaxed on the sun loungers to gaze at the night sky. And then out of nowhere, M abruptly gestured that we had to go quickly because we were being watched.

We could see a man on his motorbike in the distance lighting a cigarette and exposing his face. She said she wanted to go back to the bar, and I thought this was odd as I had already paid the bar fine. Being the nice guy I am, I made no fuss and drove her back to her bar.

Confused and really frustrated I decided to take a quiet walk along the sea front listening to the tranquil sounds of the Phuket waters with minimal street lighting to find my way. I walked up and down with a can of beer in my hands. To my horror, I was approached by a skinny looking Thai man with teeth like a lab rat. He pulled out a steak knife and threatened to stab me.

"You boom boom M?"

Shaking with his knife, he got louder and louder. It instantly occurred to me that I was being followed all that time from flirting with M in the bar to our romantic beach walk. M was aware of this, and this explains her abrupt departure. I took the Buddhist approach of calming him down. Palms open and asking him what was wrong, he told me that M was his girlfriend. I could see right away that he was madly in love with M. And all that jealously in him has built up to pull a knife out on a stranger.

I stared straight into his eyes and decided he didn't have the eyes of a really bad guy. He also didn't have the strength to dispose of my body. I was twice his size. I was tempted to disarm him. I had to slap myself across the face and remind myself that I'm not Steven Seagal and it's just easier to calm him down rather than to resorting to violence. I ended up being very open with him and assured him that I didn't know she had a boyfriend, it wasn't like she was wearing a I have a boyfriend badge or anything. He would never have understood my sarcasm and he then put his steak knife back into his pocket and drove off into the distance.

Taking a large gulp of my beer I rode back to the bar, and I explained all this to the bar owner who was an English-speaking Austrian man. He was very understanding and the next night, M had come to apologise to me. She explained that she broke up with her boyfriend before working at the bar. She then went back to my hotel room with me. I didn't have to pay any bar fine, and she didn't want any money the morning after. She was truly sorry she had put me through that experience. I don't know what M said to her ex-boyfriend, but he didn't pull a knife out on me again.

I didn't believe M's story of breaking up with her Thai boyfriend, I just enjoyed her company while it lasted. I felt bad for M's situation, how she would have to work in a bar to support her family and put her childhood sweetheart through all this jealousy.

So, for the rest of the two-week holiday, my friend and I would visit the bar daily, ring the bell and buy all the girls a drink… get some hugs and move onto the next bar. We took nothing seriously and just enjoyed the Thai bar girl experience right up to the end of our holiday.

If M's jealous ex-boyfriend didn't pull a knife out on me, I would have spent the rest of my holiday with M. I feel fortunate that I had a wake-up call with the knife experience early on while visiting Thailand so as not to let my guard completely down in the future. I'm also thankful that Thai people are humble, kind and reasonable people if you're honest with them. Everything happens for a reason, and I promised myself to never even think about bringing a bar girl to meet my parents.

****

Story 4.

You Don't Need Any Money

I love the channel and the work you do, Peter. I wanted to share this little story about an experience I had in Bangkok, I hope this story is of interest to you and your subscribers.

At the age of thirty, I upped and left my boring, single life in the UK for a year of backpacking exploring Southeast Asia. This story happened when I was about four months into my trip, I had already visited Thailand, Laos, Cambodia, Malaysia, and Vietnam for a month in each country. Whilst passing through Bangkok for the third time on this trip, I was planning to be there for three nights before making my way down to the Thai islands in the south. On the first night I went out to a few bars with a guy I had met in Vietnam a few weeks prior, he had not been to Bangkok before and was keen to see some sights.

After a day of visiting the Grand Palace and Wat Po, we found ourselves on the Khao San Road having a few beers in the bars there and ended up in a nightclub called 'The Club'. full of backpackers and young trendy types. The beers were flowing, and we were having a great night. There were a lot of local girls in this club along with young Western backpackers, there was a good vibe, loud dance music and it was very busy, everyone looked to be having fun. I was having a cigarette in one of those glass door cordoned off areas, where you can smoke. I got chatting to one of the Thai girls who was with three other friends, all in their twenties and very attractive. Most were a little shy at speaking to a farang, but the girl I got chatting to was confident and friendly. Her English was pretty much perfect, and we chain smoked a couple more cigarettes before going to the bar and getting another drink. It was all smiles, and I sensed an obvious connection between us.

Over the last four months I had only ever met Western girls from Canada, Australia and Europe who were also backpacking, so to converse with a Thai girl who spoke exceptionally good English was a refreshing change. The friend I was with just warned me to be careful as she was maybe a working girl, pickpocket, or a scammer. I was naturally quite cautious, as you should be with a stranger, having my wits about me and I wasn't too drunk.

Her flirting and talking was great and the conversation flowed naturally. We all had a dance together and continued drinking shots until the club shut. I asked what her plans were when we were out on the street, and she made it obvious that she wanted to come home with me and asked where I was staying. She said goodbye to her friends, and we walked back to my little guest house which was within walking distance from the Khao San Road. We were walking hand in hand together, grabbing some street food on the way. I decided to test the water with her status and said,

"Damn, I only have 700 Baht left."

She replied, "That's fine, you don't need any money." Which put my mind at rest.

When we got back to the guest house, the night porter started talking loudly to the girl and she handed over her ID. The conversation got a little heated and she handed over a 500 Baht note to him. When we got up to the room, I asked what happened in the reception when voices were raised, she said the security said,

"Local girls are not allowed to stay here unless they pay the hotel's joiner charge, and we treat all you working girls the same"

That made her very angry as she shouted at him, stating she was not a bar girl and in fact she was an English teacher, now I know why her English is so good. I immediately said I will give her the 500 Baht back, she replied with a smile,

"No way, I will pay this time. How about you pay tomorrow night?"

I thought this was very honest of her and we continued to have a great night together. In the morning I was quite hungover, so we arranged to see each other the next evening for food and some drinks again.

I honestly did not think she would turn up the next day, but sure enough after a lazy day of getting some washing done, checking emails and some shopping she turned up at the restaurant area of my guest house and unbelievably she was on time! I was a little taken aback but had a quick shower and got changed and ready to go out with her. We went out for some Indian food, she paid for the whole meal and now I was 100% convinced she was genuine with no hidden agenda. I insisted I pay for the rest of the night. We hit a couple of bars and shared a few cocktails, then headed back to my guest house again. The same security guard was at reception and gave us a dirty look as we walked in. I paid him the 500 Baht and walked up the stairs without saying anything. We had another great night of bedroom gymnastics and fell asleep in each other's arms until morning.

We parted ways in the morning, exchanging Facebook names and left with all smiles. What a fun couple of days it had been with no awkwardness, or any mention of money being exchanged.

The next day I flew down to Krabi and continued on my trip. We never saw each other again but kept in touch via Facebook, I saw on her profile that she was previously married to an Englishman, but now divorced and it was plain to me that she only liked Western men. This assured me that she had a professional career and that simply Western men were her type.

When I visit Thailand now, I preach that you can meet genuine Thai girls, not every one of them is a money grabber or a working girl out to fleece you.

We occasionally keep in touch now and it's around ten years later, messaging a few times a year to catch up and laugh about the time we spent together. She is now with a European man, and they look to be very happy together.

I am now married off with kids, but fondly remember my little fling with a genuine Thai girl. Thanks, and keep up the good work on the channel and best wishes with the move over to Thailand.

****

Story 5.

Catching the Thailand Bug

This was my very first trip to Thailand. It was going to be the same story as many other guys. I had been married for eighteen years, worked hard, and done my best for my family then everything fell apart. I'm divorced now and was wondering what the hell had happened. I got invited to come along to Thailand with a guy from work who has been numerous times and knows the ropes apparently. I did some research before heading out to Thailand.

I arrived in Pattaya not knowing what to expect but got a big awakening what with the all the bars, girls, and Go-Go bars. Believe it or not, I met the Thai love of my life in Spider girl bar. She had just arrived from her village and could hardly speak English, but we just clicked. I found out her name was Nan and ended up staying with her and giving her 2,000 Baht for her time.

Everybody had warned me about falling for a bar girl, but I did fall for her, I really liked her. I found out later that she had a Thai husband. She told me that she had been working as a cook because she wanted to save money to have her daughter educated properly, she had saved quite a bit over time, but her husband demanded the money one day telling her he wanted to buy a new car. She went on to tell me that as she'd been saving for a long time for her daughter's school fees, she flatly refused to hand over the money, so he shot his wife in the leg and stole her money anyway which explained the scar on her leg. Apparently, this is why she ended up working in the bar to make fast money to try and recoup the money for her daughter's education.

All good things must come to an end, and it was time for me to go home. I went to her bar to say goodbye, she wanted to stay with me on my last night, but I explained that I didn't have enough money to pay the bar fine, so she offered to pay the bar fine herself. How could I refuse an offer like that! I took her up on her offer and she came back with me on my last night in Pattaya. We had a brilliant night together and I promised I'd be back soon. Yes, I had been bitten by the Thailand bug and yes, I was quite naïve but in my defence, I would say remember,

"This was my first time in the Land of Smiles."

In the end I ended up giving her 1600 baht and I was left with virtually nothing but good memories. I put her in a baht bus and sent her back to central Pattaya as I was staying in Jomtien on this trip. At this point I was feeling quite emotional but told myself this was all part of that Thailand game.

Now this next bit might be a bit hard to swallow but I swear this really happened. After putting her in the back of the bus I was walking back to my hotel, I put my hands in my pockets and discovered she had secretly slid the money I had given her into my pocket. so basically, she left with nothing, did she really like me?

On my next trip to Pattaya I went straight to her bar, she wasn't there, and I was told that the bar scene wasn't for her, and she had gone back to her village. To this day I still believe she was a decent girl with good intentions. I wish I could go back seven years to meet her knowing what I know now. I still think about her often, fantastic memories of my first love in Thailand. I hope the world is treating her right and I hope she is happy.

****

Story 6.

Lose Face?
Cats Will Fight

My story takes place well after being a now seasoned veteran of Thailand and this story took place on maybe my sixth or seventh trip in two years. I had met a girl from a quiet beer-bar near my condo in Jomtien that I used to pop into at the end of most nights on the way home. It was quite a small bar but there were several pretty girls working in this bar, I met one who I quite took to.

The girl was called Pong and I'd spent time with her on several different evenings. Pong had mentioned that she'd love to come back to England with me as I had been up country to visit her family. I thought I was by now very experienced, but it seems I was greener than I thought. I had met her on a previous trip and had been sending her a monthly allowance so that her kids could go to school, and she could buy medicine for her sick Buffalo.

When I was back home, I would call Pong daily. Whenever I spoke with her there was something not quite right, I don't know what it was but there was something I could just sense it.

There's an old saying that says, "trust your own instincts."

Well at the time I was working for myself, so I decided to jump on a plane and fly out to Thailand to see for myself. When I arrived at Pong's small bar, all of the girls just froze and looked at me in what appeared to be disbelieve!

Remember the advert for woodpecker cider years ago where the whole bar stops, goes quiet and stares, well this is what it felt like to me.

The cashier came over and steered me to the far end of the bar and sat me down. Next, who should appear but my darling Tilak on the arm of an old guy. I wasn't completely surprised but the guy must have been eighty and not the sharpest tool in the box. He was the only person in the bar that wasn't aware of the situation.

Pong was dumbstruck she had been caught out. It turns out she was living with this guy; he was spending a fortune on her. I didn't make a scene, if she wanted to be with him that was fine by me. I thought I will just walk away with my head held high and told myself to just move on to the next bar and its new possibilities.

I didn't walk away instead I stayed in the bar drinking mainly to make life uncomfortable for her if I'm honest. At about eight o'clock Pong and the old guy said good night to everyone and left the bar, so I thought that was the end of the night's entertainment but no, about an hour later Pong come backs to the bar with her sister and straight over to me. After some attempted yak yak by Pong, BS basically, I told her she can't have us both. She needs to either choose the old guy or me. I went on to tell her I didn't care either way, if she thought he was better than me that's fine, choose him and I'll walk away, plenty of fish in the sea, right?

I think this part of the story is going to be quite predictable because we ended up drinking together for the remainder of the evening and at the end of the night my judgment being clouded by alcohol, Pong ended up in my room once again. We ended up having a great night of aerobics. She told me that the old guy couldn't manage it any longer and she had really enjoyed the night with me.

The whole situation got into a really weird routine! Pong would stay with the old guy all day; he would take her shopping, buy her food then they would come to the bar for a couple of drinks early. They would both go home because he was tired, she would then head back out to meet me at her bar. After a while and after brooding for a while, I took the decision to tell Pong to stay with the other guy and take care of him! I just didn't like this situation any longer, it was a novelty at first, but the novelty soon wore thin quickly.

I went back to being young free and single again, well free and single maybe. I met another girl in a bar who I really liked and was quite nice. I decided I wanted to take her out of the bar and let her show me around like a tourist as I really liked her company. She agreed so we decided on a trip to Ayutthaya. It was a great trip and I think she had a great time looking at the temples and being away from the bar scene.

I remember one day thinking to myself, 'Everything in the world is now good. Pong has her boyfriend, and I am with an even nicer girl who I really like.'

This new girl was called "Jip." I stayed with Jip for the remainder of my holiday. One point I forgot to mention in this story is that Jip worked in the same bar as Pong. One day Jip and I are having a quiet drink alone in the bar when who should walk in but Pong and her sister and a third girl they knew! The next thing I know is that Pong and the other two girls attack Jip. I don't know why but it was quite vicious, but I did manage to break it up. I remember thinking at the time, if this is because Pong is jealous of Jip, she's got a hell of a nerve because I caught her red handed with the old guy and yet here, she was playing the victim. Anyway, it all seemed to quieten down and I said to Jip, "Let's leave."

Jip and I left the bar and walked up the Soi when everything had calmed down. I couldn't believe what happened next. Pong came running up the Soi, jumped on Jip and the pair of them ended up rolling around in the dirt fighting.

Pong's sister and her friend tried to hold me back so that I couldn't intervene and stop the fight. The next thing I see is police turning up out of nowhere. They turned out to be the tourist police and one of them said to me,

"Look, I would leave this area quickly if I was you."

I said, "It's not me fighting, why should I run away?"

He said, "Because you're involved, the regular police will arrest you and take you to the police station."

Again, I asked him why I should leave I've done nothing wrong? He basically explained to me that if I hadn't have gotten the plane and come to Thailand this wouldn't have happened. So, it's my fault, that's how they look at it… Don't you just love the logic?

I took his advice and let them sort it out by themselves. I kept a low profile for the rest of this trip and took Jip to Krabi the next trip.

I learnt a valuable lesson though. It's all about not losing face in Thailand! Although Pong didn't really care if she was with me or not, the fact that I took another girl out of the same bar made her lose face in front of all the other girls in the bar, so she had to seek revenge on Jip, again, that's just how it is in Thailand.

With all of what I have explained here, I still have a fantastic time every time I visit Thailand and yes, meeting up with Jip is on the agenda for my next trip.

Story 7.

The Spirit of Music

I first came to Thailand almost by accident in 1994 I was forty-three. I had a thing about girls of colour and at the time was booked to go to the Gambia again, but as there were some riots in Banjul, the capital. The British Government was recommending people not to visit, so I changed the booking for three nights in Bangkok and ten days in Pattaya for Christmas.

I stayed in the Asia Hotel in Bangkok, in the foyer they had photos of Muhammad Ali when he stayed there and other famous guests. It was my first experience of what became my main interest in Thailand, they had a music cafe, more like a nightclub with singers, and the waitresses in long traditional skirts knelt down to serve you drinks. I remember thinking at the time the singers were terrible! Out as soon as possible to

Patpong with a guy on the tour, a double-glazing salesman from Derby named Sid. I had read all about rip off bars upstairs, but we never had any problems and after those with the erotic shows we ended up in the Touch bar, which was offering an all-in service on the premises, it was on a sign behind the bar. One nice girl tried to make me accept this offer I could not refuse, but like an idiot I did!

Onto the Lime-Light bar where Sid hooked up with a girl, this place looked a bit more respectable. We went back to the hotel, and I did not see Sid until the next morning. He was really pissed off, the girl had refused to do any more than drink with Sid in the room but still wanted paying for her time, his double-glazing sales technique could not get her to change her mind.

Onto Pattaya, which for some reason I imagined would still be like a fishing village, but with a few hotels and bars. Even by this time it was very built up with little planning, the roads stank of sewage, and it was quite unattractive.

Most people on the tour had a look round and went to travel agents to book trips elsewhere. I stayed and had quite a miserable time despite going out every night. Soi Diamond was my favourite place which had a round revolving bar in the middle and 'Super Baby Ago-go' where I bar fined my first girl, Lek from Pitsanalook, or so she claimed, had never met any other girl from there. It's central Thailand not Issan where most Pattaya bar workers come from. I didn't have a very nice session with this girl, and I think we were back in the bar within forty minutes. I gave her far too much money when she said up to you. I arranged to meet her the next day at lunchtime, but she did not turn up. That was the highlight really, I did not bar fine anymore and ended up just wishing I had gone to Ko Chang with Sid, but we did spend a nice Christmas day 1994 in Bang Saan, far nicer than Pattaya and not changed that much today.

I met a girl giving massages on Jomtien beach one day and arranged to meet her at the Marine disco later. After a couple of hours there buying her and her friends drinks, I was running low on cash so told her I was nipping back to the hotel for some money. When I got back about thirty minutes later, she was just leaving with another guy! Overall, I really did not have a good time and decided there was no way I would ever be going back to Thailand.

One thing I did do in Pattaya, with nothing much else to do, was buy some Thai music tapes from a woman on a bike with a collection on a stand. I had no idea what to get so just bought three with the nicest looking women on the covers. One was string style which soon went in the bin, but the others turned out to be two great singers of luktung and lukrung musical styles. I was to meet them years later in the future.

I went to Pattaya again a few years later, booked in a hotel for a week but left again back to Bangkok the next day, I just did not like the place at all. After that, I visited a few times but only for an evening to see a concert, including the Pattaya music festival.

Back home four months later the first Thai take away opened just around the corner and I was soon in there every day, then helping the owner Nan, followed by getting into a relationship with her. At first, I did not know she was married, then came the tales of her husband not being good to her. She had been in the UK with this guy Martin for five years, in Thailand she had been married very young and was in the Air Force. She told me she shot her first husband when she found out he was cheating on her, luckily, he did not die!

Oh yes when I did meet Martin, he was one of the nicest guys you could imagine so I felt a bit guilty and was pretty sure she had lied about him cheating on her.

She encouraged me to sell my flat and buy a house not far away. The plan was for her to leave Martin and help with the mortgage. Also, her sister and niece were to be moved in, which they did for a short time.

Two months after moving in and waiting for her, Martin got cancer, so she changed her mind, obviously she's thinking of inheriting the house, which does happen. Martin died the next year.

Despite promising him to look after the house along with his Siamese cats, and look after his two kids financially, she sold the lot and moved away as soon as possible having lined up another sponsor, her reason to me why we could not be together. She could not be with anyone who had less then she now had! I actually went to Thailand with her and her family a couple of times, once to have Martin's ashes put in the wall at a Wat in Nakon Nayok, where they were from. One thing I recall on the trip was Nan showing me a Gucci watch the new boyfriend had bought her which cost several hundred pounds, quite a bit in 1998, but moaning it was no good as it did not have a gold strap! It's not just bar girls who are materialistic.

I started going to Go-Go bars in Thailand two to three times a year, but often thought never again, but always at the last minute I'd meet somebody interesting to get me back there. There was a psychic, Ann from the Thermae coffee shop with her ghost stories and supernatural experiences. Cake from Clinton Plaza who became a friend, Sudjai from Tilak bar in Soi Cowboy whose services were outstanding! The amazingly gorgeous Dao who had a bar called Barbies on Asok corner, then it was a cleared away to make room for a building site through to Sukhumvit Soi 23. Ann had been a singer at Thonburi Cafe on the other side of the river until the crash in 1997.

Although she was poor at the special activities, she made up for it with her stories and personality. One night we were in a gloomy Chinese hotel on Sukhumvit Soi 8 which looked like it had never been renovated since the sixties. She said she was very cold which was odd as it was hot there being no air con in this room. She explained it was her 'friend.' I said what friend? She told me she had a friend who had died from HIV a few years before and she went to her funeral up country. She heard her friend's spirit was confused and did not know where to go. Ann said she told her to go back with her to Bangkok, which was what happened. Ann said her friend tells her who the bad guys are and who to avoid in Thermae. She said she does not see her, but feels her,

"Is she here now," I asked.

"Yes!" replied Ann.

She also told me about when she did see a spirit and it split her up with a boyfriend. She was keen on a Canadian at one time but when they were alone, she often saw a spirit watching in the room. In the end the guy asked what was wrong, so she told him, and he asked her to describe what the spirit looked like. Turned out to be his best friend who had died in a car crash several years ago. She said the stress was too great, so she had to end that relationship. I always thought they were just stories maybe to avoid special activities until one night when I decided to avoid her. She always sat in the same place at the front just as you came down the stairs, and I always went in this way. But there was another way in through the toilet area at the back so one night I went in there having walked the short way up the Soi from my hotel.

I was shocked to see her waiting there as soon as I stepped in from the Soi. I asked her what she was up to?

"Waiting for you," she said.

"Why here? I asked.

She said the friend had told her I was coming in that way and there was no way somebody could have told her; this was before we all had mobiles. It was late, so I said I thought she would have met somebody. Yes, she told me she had a few offers but was waiting for me. That was this night sorted then! With Dao, I sometimes went to a music cafe upstairs where Terminal 21 is now. If you think girls like the music played in bars for Westerners, they almost never do. I saw two semi-famous singers, good luktung singers both dead now.

About this time, I started going to music cafes, the first one had been near Rangsit, it was called the Big Shrimp. One night a visiting girl Robce Troupe came on stage and the highlight of their act was to rip off their costumes and to be stark naked briefly. They and the singers would sit with customers, especially if you bought them a Mali, an artificial or real flower necklace often with money attached. I thought, well this is far more entertaining than bars and a Go-Go's, as well as a lot cheaper. Tankey Issan on Rachada was the best cafe, they have almost all gone today. At Tankey you could buy a book of tickets to dance with girls there, ridiculously cheap, give the girl a ticket and off you went, better than having to buy lady drinks.

Far too much about cafes to tell, sometimes singers, some very famous would invite you to eat after a concert or to their home for a party. Over the years I went to well over a thousand concerts in Thailand, apart from visiting cafes and music pubs and have seen all the well-known singers, one female artist one hundred and forty times!

The music scene was by far the most fun I have ever had in Thailand. Eventually I thought I had better start learning some Thai, so I enrolled at Somchart language school Sukhumvit, Bangkok in 2002 and had a few lessons, paid 7,000 Baht upfront and the owner told me it was valid for two years. I never got back until a year later when she told me it was only a year and that ran out last week. No paperwork, so she cheated me out of the 7,000 Baht. I was really keen on my little teacher but as she had left, I was not too upset at this nasty little scam. How to find my cute teacher Lek again?

Luckily somebody knew her on a Thai forum, so he gave me her number and we arranged to meet up for lessons. She was also a big country music fan but as well as Luktung and Morlam she liked Kantrum as well as she's from Surin. Their language and music have its roots in Cambodia who ruled large parts of Thailand hundreds of years ago. Lek's favourite singer was a very famous Kantrum performer called Darkie, he's passed away now but would probably have to change his name today!

At this time, I had a girlfriend who I had met two years before in a Hua Hin bar called Hogs Breath, and she was from Krasang, Buri Ram. We had gone home to meet her parents the year before, but her father hated foreigners and although he was a Tuk Tuk driver he refused to pick us up at the station. This was one thing that put me off her a little, but we did talk about getting married and she was keen, she was now working at MBK then at a hotel.

At one time I gave her a bank card and told her to take out a fixed amount every month but no more. But she could not resist taking money out every week, so I stopped that, another minus point there. There were others, when I told her I was going to buy her a good second-hand car when she came over after we were married, she said she did not want a car, she wanted a house, presumably for her mum, who already had one, that was a big con, I don't think so.

Teacher Lek had been ringing round to find a good concert to see on Christmas day 2003, it was much harder than before the internet really took off here. She found a good one at a Wat on Sukhumvit 101, with famous singers from Korat, they were always on TV and these days as a judge on the singing contests.

Once I was at a packed M105 concert outside at night and gave her a Mali of orchids after a song. She heard some negative remark in the crowd and told them off, she told them I knew more about Thai music than most Thais did, always love her. I invited teacher Lek to come with us. While the concert was great, and I got to meet Sunaree for the first time the feathers flew after with Lek accusing me of having a thing for Sunaree. I had not really thought of her in that way.

In the end Lek and I did not get married. The other lady had a guy on the back burner anyway and got married in 2004 the year before I did and moved to the USA with her daughter. I married my Thai teacher instead. I still cannot speak Thai very well though, but I can afford the lessons!

****

Story 8.

Full Moon Party

This story took place in the New Year between 2015 and 2016. I was twenty-six and had been living in Thailand for two years. My best friend from back home in the UK, Pete was visiting. Pete had already been to Thailand once and loved it.

He arrived early in the morning on Christmas Eve, and we met up at the Nana hotel. We got rooms, ditched the bags, and jumped straight into the pool where we chilled and caught up. At one point, a freelancer approached us at the poolside, showing some very X-rated videos with men including one video where she had golf balls popping out of a place where golf balls shouldn't be! She asks if either of us want to go with her and while it was an interesting offer, ultimately, we declined. We still laugh about the story of the golf ball girl to this day.

Later, we got burgers then we hit the bars. We started at Hanrahan's, the Irish pub on Soi 4 before going to Hillary opposite the Nana Hotel. Later, we end up in Nana Plaza in a Go-Go bar called London Calling, with lots of girls walking around while not wearing very much. One takes my fancy. She's a gorgeous little lady with a pretty face, red bikini, and blonde highlights. She approaches me, introducing herself as Daeng from Udon Thani. Pete is soon joined by another of the dancers. I ended up bar fining her, giving a head nod to Pete and his girl as we departed. I get Daeng back to my room where we enjoyed each other's company. Woke up Christmas Day and Daeng leaves. We exchange Line IDs with the vague intention of seeing each other again before saying goodbye.

Pete and I just spent the day lazing by the pool and ended up in Hillary bar again that night. There, we saw two attractive girls across the room who smile at us. One is in a black dress with jet black hair while the other is a petite girl in a red dress with bleached blonde hair. So, we wandered over to chat to them. They were teachers from the Philippines, no wonder their English was so good. Pete hits it off with the girl in the black dress, named Veronica while I get close with the red dress girl, named Cindy. Later we end up back in my room where the drinks continue. Veronica then takes Pete, and they go back to his room next door, and I'm left alone with Cindy and I'm sure you don't need me to explain the rest. Merry Christmas from Bangkok! I love Filipina girls.

The next morning at breakfast, Pete looks tense and when outside of earshot of the girls, he tells me that Veronica is annoying and has already become clingy.

The girls tell us they want to hang out with us, but we pretended we were leaving town that day. I like Cindy so I become friends with her on Facebook, but Pete can't get away from Veronica. I vaguely plan to see Cindy sometime and we say our goodbyes. We were soon to travel to the New Year beach party in Koh Phangyan.

There were no flights at the time, so we ended up taking the slow train which turned out to be a great choice as you'll learn later.

On the day it was time to travel, we met my two friends from Pattaya, Rob and

Phil at the main train station in Bangkok. Rob was an Aussie, a year younger than me and probably my best friend in Thailand. The other guy, Phil, was an American in his 30s. He loved the ladies and was your typical 'Pattaya farang.' I was glad to see that Pete and the two guys hit it off immediately and we became quite the squad. It was a local train, with wooden seats, no air-conditioning, and a funky smell. We departed Bangkok and seemed to travel very slowly.

Soon after leaving Bangkok, we hear the chatter of several Europeans coming into our carriage. With plenty of space nearby, we invite them to join us, and they do. There's four guys and two girls, looking to be in their mid-twenties. They are Italian and German and have just been studying in Bangkok and are heading to the full moon party, then Phuket before they go back to their countries.

My attention was immediately caught by one of the girls. Being in Asia for so long, I haven't dated a Western girl for a long time, but this girl was stunning. She had dark hair, striking blue eyes and a glorious tan that only comes from several months in Southeast Asia.

We start talking and she introduces herself as Isabella, a 23-year-old from

Northern Italy. She speaks fluent English with a British accent as she studied in Brighton a couple of years prior. She was very likeable, and I quickly developed a crush on her. We talked for the entire thirteen hours, through the night as everyone else slept and right till our arrival in Surat Thani early in the morning. We then travelled together by boat to Koh Samui. Upon arrival, we separated as me and the guys had a night in Koh Samui while the Europeans were heading directly to Koh Phangyan.

After we parted ways, it immediately hit me that I had forgotten to get Isabella's contact. No phone number or social media. Gutted, I liked this girl. We stayed in a grubby, cheap guesthouse in Chaweng beach, and chilled on the beach that day. I wasn't in the mood to go out that night. The tiredness from the train journey had caught up with me so I stayed in as the guys went out.

The next morning, we caught the boat across to Koh Phangyan. Through poor travel planning, every single motorbike on the island had already been rented. We walked the streets in frustration till we found someone renting out a Toyota Hilux pickup truck. We drove the truck through jungle tracks to our beach bungalows. Got there, ditched our bags and dived, headfirst into the idyllic, blue sea. If there was a paradise, it must be here.

We bought a plastic Frisbee and a kid's football and just chilled on the beach for the day. That night, we head over to Haad Rin where the Full Moon Party was being held. I've never seen anything like it before. It was massive, stretching from one corner of the beach to the other, with huge crowds and lights as far as I could see. The noise was tremendous, and hundreds of speakers blasted every kind of music on top of each other. We bought mysterious concoctions of alcohol, coke and red bull sold in little children's plastic buckets. Times were good and a couple of hours passed in a blur.

Suddenly, I was tapped on the shoulder from behind and heard a familiar voice say my name. I turned around and was very surprised, there was Isabella, the Italian girl from the train along with the German girl she was with before. Her other friends were nowhere to be seen. We hugged and exclaimed shock and surprise of seeing each other again on this huge beach with literally thousands of revellers, what were the odds?!

We exchanged Facebooks, laughing at the sheer randomness of the situation. The next couple of hours passed in a flash and before long, it was the countdown to midnight. Five, four, three, two, one. Fireworks and music blasted as the clock struck twelve. We admired the view and I looked at Isabella. She was stunning in her neon party attire and glowing face paint. She smiled at me, then kissed me passionately. We partied the night away and Rob got very close with Isabella's German friend. Pete and Phil had wandered off into the chaos and were nowhere to be seen. 3am came and tiredness sets in. I text Pete and Phil telling them we want to leave. Pete tells me him and Phil had found a couple of Thai girls and would stay with them for the night. Myself, Rob, Isabella, and her German friend get into the truck, ears ringing from the noise.

I'm not a big drinker and felt fine enough to drive back. Isabella sat up front with me while Rob and the German girl made out in the back. Back to the Bungalows, Rob, and the German in one and Isabella and I in the other, and you can guess the rest. I wake as the sun peeks through the curtains with Isabella still asleep.

Happy New Year.

Outside later, we find Rob and the German girl talking and we join them. We spent that day chilling by the sea. I felt like I was living in Alex Garland's The Beach.

At some point later, Pete and Phil came back, looking worse for wear but grinning like Cheshire cats after their night with the two Thai girls. That night, we went to a pool party that the girls had invited us to. There, we caught up with the guys who they had travelled with and partied until I went back to Isabella's room nearby so that Pete and Phil could sleep in my bungalow undisturbed while Rob and the German girl stayed in the other bungalow. Isabella and I talked and enjoyed our time together that night as we would be parting ways in the morning as they went to Phuket while we were going back to Bangkok.

In the morning, we made some vague promises to see each other again even though we both knew it wouldn't happen. Such as it is with the innocence of young romance. Rob picked me up in the truck as he brought the German girl back. As sad as I was to be leaving the party, I felt happy that I still had another week of holiday with Pete ahead.

We returned the pickup truck and went by boat to Chumpon on the mainland before catching a bus back to Bangkok. We arrived at night and checked in to a cheap hotel near the Victory Monument. We were not in the mood for partying so just got some food before sleeping.

The next morning, we took a crazy minivan ride for two hours down to Pattaya. I had an apartment there, but Pete offered to get me a room in the same hotel he was staying at which I couldn't refuse. The next few days were a blur of chilling by day and typical Pattaya antics by night.

Eventually, Pete's last day came before he needed to head back to Bangkok to catch his flight back to the UK. That night, we just stayed in the hotel, sitting on his balcony with a few cans of beer and talked. It was really sad to see Pete leave but he felt worse. I was lucky enough to be living in Pattaya while he had to head back to dreary old England.

Morning came and we said goodbye to Pete as we go back to our normal lives. I get a message a few days later from Pete telling me he's in England and he wishes he was back. A few days later, Isabella sends me a selfie in the snowy, alpine mountains of Northern Italy. Cindy messaged me asking if Pete will call

Veronica as she needs money…Not likely.

****

Story 9.

Loopy Copper

Back in 2013, I was twenty-four and had been teaching in Thailand for a couple of months and was still fairly new to everything. My supervisor was a Thai woman called Loop, who was a couple of years my senior. I'd hung out with Loop a few times and we ended up dating for around a year. The relationship fizzled out after I moved schools, but we wished each other well.

Loop was a government teacher with the body "Kru Sapa" (ministry of education). Anyone who has taught in Thailand will be familiar with "government teachers" as they wear the brown military uniforms to school on Mondays and get quite a lot of benefits. Loop was rather powerful in my school and was well known in the town I lived in.

PETER HOPKINS

One day, I was travelling down a highway on my motorbike and was stopped at a red light with around ten other bikes. Being Thailand, people ran the red light without a care in the world. When the light turned green, I continued and about fifty metres ahead, there was a group of brown-uniformed traffic policemen stopping people on bikes. One of them steps out into the road ahead of me, singles me out of the crowd and gestures me to pull over, which I did. Dollar signs flashed in his eyes as he targeted the lone, tasty farang on the road. He then starts asking me about documents and licenses which I, as many young teachers in Thailand at the time, didn't have. As annoyed as I was for being singled out among the crowd of careless Thai drivers, I was more scared as I knew the heavy punishments in the UK for driving without documents and was still new to Thailand.

He started laying it on thick about how much trouble I was in and that I would need to pay 4000 Baht. As a poor teacher, 4000 Baht was a lot to me at the time. I acted dumb and put on my thickest Yorkshire accent in the hopes of confusing the guy, but he didn't relent. I then did the next best thing and called

Loop, asking for help. She told me she wanted to speak to him, so I handed my phone over. After a quick thirty second phone call which the cop saying "Krup" (yep yep), his face dropped and he hung up the phone, handing it back to me and frustratedly saying, "Goodbye."

He didn't get a penny out of me and to this day I have no idea what Loop told him although I think it was something along the lines of,

"He's one of my teachers, we have connections with the provincial office, could you please cut him some slack." Although in truth I'll never know.

I figured if there was one metaphor for Thailand and the corruption situation in the country, this story was it.

****

Story 10.

Amazing Massage

My name is Tom and I have a short story about something that happened to me in Thailand back in 2006 to share with you and hopefully your viewers and readers. You can use my name as I have nothing to hide with this story as it's one, I have told my friends many times before.

I was a naive 28-year-old travelling around Asia with my then fiancée Lisa who was 21. It was our first trip ever to the Land of Smiles, first of many (for me). I know you have mentioned this in many other stories previously, but there really are no words to describe that feeling you get as soon as you step off the aircraft in Bangkok. The smells, that intense heat, the humidity and the brightness of the sun. After an eleven-hour flight, stuck in an air-conditioned, cramped up economy seat, your senses are simply overload.

After a long, slow process through customs, passport control, luggage collection, and rush hour taxi to your Bangkok hotel, that rush of cold blood soon becomes a distant memory, the jet-lag kicks in and you want nothing more than to fall into a deep sleep in your hotel room. But you know you can't as it's only 6pm and if you sleep now you will wake at around 2am, everything will be closed and that's no way to start a holiday.

Lisa suggested we go for a walk, and I agreed this was probably the best way to deal with the tiredness. Maybe we could get some food and have a drink on the river. Not far from our hotel we were approached by a lady in her fifties.

"Massage for you?" She enquired.

I was shy and politely declined, but Lisa thought it would be a great way to relax without going to sleep. And at 300 Baht it sounded like a bargain, so she said yes.

I really didn't fancy being rubbed with oil by a lady in her fifties for two hours so I told Lisa that I would have a drink and wait for her. I went to a bar opposite near the location and Lisa agreed to meet me there after her massage. I don't remember the name of the bar, but this is what I would later learn to be a typical Thai beer bar full of beautiful girls looking for men to buy them lady drinks and everything else they provided for a fee.

Being inexperienced and generally not interested in additional female company I must say that the girls in the bar were incredibly warm and very friendly. I told them about Lisa and explained that she was having a massage across the street and would meet me here when she was done.

Over the next two hours I had a few beers and was joking with the girls; I even bought several lady drinks for two of the ladies who decided to join me at my table, perhaps out of boredom. The jet lag had passed, I was in high spirits and now in a great holiday mood. After a while, one of the girls joked,

"Your girlfriend not come, you take me home instead."

I laughed but then looked at my watch and it had been well past two hours, maybe close to thirty minutes past and I thought that was strange. I paid my bill, waved goodbye and left the bar.

It was dark now, but the lights of Bangkok made the streets look brighter than ever. I looked through the window of the massage shop but couldn't see Lisa inside. I decided to go inside and look for her.

"Take off shoe, take off shoe," said an old lady, pointing at my feet.

"No, I don't want a massage; I am looking for my girlfriend."

"Take off shoe, then you come in," she replied.

"I am looking for my girlfriend."

"Yes, you have to take off shoe before you come in."

I took off my shoes and socks and placed them by a pile of sandals at the door.

"You need girlfriend?" the lady asked.

"Yes," came my reply.

"You wait here, I bring for you."

'Finely' I thought, as the lady disappeared.

Maybe Lisa fell asleep after the massage, and they didn't want to wake her. Five minutes later the lady came back with five other ladies from upstairs. We have nice girlfriends for you, as she introduces me to the girls.

"No, no, you don't understand. I am looking for my girlfriend she was here earlier. She is much younger than these ladies," I joked.

The lady dismissed the five women who went back upstairs and started shouting in Thai. Then about a minute later a younger girl came downstairs, maybe 24 years old.

"You can take this lady with you for looking Bangkok and up to you everything."

I felt my face beam red with embarrassment, and I genuinely started to worry about what had happened to Lisa.

I looked over at the shoes and picked up Lisa's trainers.

"These girlfriend's shoe., She came here for a massage over two hours ago, where has she gone?"

"Oh, she upstairs, you say girlfriend, I think you wanted new lady," she laughed. "You go up you will see her at end of corridor."

I walked up the staircase. The nice and clean interior of the welcoming downstairs reception didn't extend past this point. The walls were damp and sodden. The staircase was rotting, and I was too nervous to use the handrail for fear of it falling off in my hand and getting the bill to repair it. This place wasn't nice. The first room I walked past had just a dirty mattress on the floor and a shower. The girls that visited me downstairs were all in the adjacent room eating food from bags with plastic cutlery. Where was Lisa?

I made my way down the long corridor. I saw a syringe on the floor,

'I hope that's for insulin,' I thought.

Then I saw Lisa, face down on the mattress, half naked and not moving. A second rush of cold blood, for my first day in Thailand, but this time it wasn't excitement, it was fear. I tapped Lisa lightly, still nothing. I sat her up and said her name again,

"Lisa, wake up." She woke up.

"Wow that was amazing," she said. "What time is it?"

"Late," I replied, relieved.

Lisa being jet lagged had fallen asleep during the massage and they decided to let her rest. She had no idea so much time had passed. We paid 300 Baht and left.

****

Story 11.

Changing Times

I first visited Bangkok in the 1980's on a visit to Indonesia and Burma but Bangkok is where I transferred, and I had a few days there and I was hooked on Thailand. The following year I took a longer trip to Thailand and visited a lot of the ancient cities as my interest back then was history, rather than beer and bars. I have never been to Pattaya, and I was a poor young backpacker at that time. I treated myself to just one soapy massage before flying home.

On the next trip I stayed in a very cheap hotel in Chinatown where I have to say, I first experienced a stuffed omelette for breakfast, very strange. Anyway, I visited a souvenir shop run by a girl called Nah to get postcards as mementos and I got on friendly terms with Nah.

I was very surprised when Nah turned up at my hotel and invited me to stay with her family. Of course, that sounded a wonderful idea. In fact, I saw little of Nah, as she was working very long hours and it was her brother I was mostly with when they took me up to the rice farm in Issan. I got to see a lot of places and I was also introduced to Issan food, sticky rice balls and raw cow stomach. Sometimes I would eat at a local Thai eating place on the grass verge which made the best Pad Thai that I have ever had. Unfortunately, on the second visit we had a plague of flying ants that shed lots of ant wings over all over the food. I learned a very important Thai custom on that day,

"Say nothing, and pretend it isn't happening."

I fixed the house lights once when the fuse blew, for some reason they didn't know about fuses, and then I was off to the airport. Nah asked if I was going back to London and I said,

"No, Burma."

"You got friend there?" She asked.

"Yes?"

"Boy or girl?"

"Girl." And then it came out, I had to use a quote from Lord of the Rings!

"There is nothing that hurts a man more than having to reject the love of a fine woman that can't be returned."

So, I will jump ahead now from the 1980's to the 1990's when Thailand was coming out of third world insurgency, where it was rather like Cambodia in the 90's, and becoming an Asian tiger with a Metro system. Bangkok had changed! The souvenir shop where I had met Nah had gone. Patpong was no longer as exciting as it had been in the past. Nana Plaza and Soi Cowboy were now the more popular areas to spend the evening for single guys out for fun.

I still visited a Kobe steak place that I always liked when passing through Patpong and I would pop into some of the bars for a drink although I'm not a big drinker, it was more for old times' sake before going back to my favourite bars in Nana and Soi Cowboy. In Soi 8 Nana I can recommend 'The Bamboo Bar'. I went once and was hooked. The girl behind the desk explained

"You can have any of the girls. You can have me, up to you."

In the end I hooked up with a nice girl called, Ging (which means branch, in Thai). It was more a GF experience than most massage or bar girl encounters I'd had in the past. Some girls give fake smiles but I'd' rather have a nice smile than a miserable looking girl with me.

I was at my favourite bar in Soi Cowboy, which was great fun before it all declined in quality, with more covering up, deafening music, the young dudes with their baseball caps on back to front, telling me,

"If it's too loud, you're too old," and of course, higher prices.

You had to watch these bars for scams back then. In fact, some bars were closed down by the Police for a while for scamming foreigners.

I could maybe give you that story but maybe another day.

But it was good for entertaining a girl before showing her the contents of your hotel mini bar. It flatters the ego of an old Monger to have a very pretty girl fling herself at him as soon as he finds his way through the door.

Back at the bar I sat and looked over a few rotations of the stage while sipping Chang and watching a pretty girl that had been pulled off stage by an old guy. She was wriggling to free herself from his clutches and seemed not at all happy about his freebie groping. So, she waved goodbye to him with a smile so as not to cause offence.

One girl was made up to look like an American blond; a small part actress that the Mama-san offered me. Why do they think guys want to come to Thailand and find a girl who looks like what they left behind, I have no idea?

I saw that the pretty girl had escaped, her molester had left, and she was now back on stage doing the 'bar-girl shuffle.' She was talking to another girl on stage that looked similar to her. Well, that was too good to miss so I waved them over to join me, first having them sit together as they were still wary after Jabber the Hut had been manhandling one of them and chatted without bothering them, getting them drinks so they loosened up and relaxed and revealed they were twin sisters (I had come across a surprising number of those in my time visiting Bangkok - obviously it attracts customers). After their shift, they sat each side and I ended up bar fining both of them. The moral of the story being "If two girls is too much, you're too young."

****

Story 12.

My Go-to Place

Hi Peter, I'm John, a 42-year-old man from a town called Shirebrook near Mansfield in the East Midlands. I'd firstly like to say how much me and my friend Ray like listening to all your stories.

My story is a rather long one as I've been going to Thailand since November 2009 and obviously back then I was just a 30-year-old. It was the time of the financial crisis and as I'm a self-employed plasterer there wasn't a lot of work around due to the housing market slowing down with the banks not lending much money for mortgages at this time.

I was working in Mansfield at the time in a fire door production factory. I'd recently broke up from a long-term relationship in 2007, feeling a little insecure and very bored with this factory job I had. A few of my new found work friends at the factory were also wanting a little more from life other than making fire doors for a living in boring Mansfield.

We all regularly chatted about getting a work visa for another country and leaving this dull factory life behind. All four of us decided we wanted to go to Australia and work, so we applied for a working holiday visa, and we all got accepted. I was very excited about the whole new experience I was going to have, and I started doing some research about having a holiday stop on the way. One of the guys had already been to Thailand before but not for a long period and had told me a few stories about the Kingdom. Our departure date of November the 9th 2009 had finely arrived. We flew Thai Airways, three of us had never flown long haul before so we made the most of it with the free drinks and food onboard.

We met a guy on the aircraft also going to Thailand but with a lot more experience than us. He told us lots of stories about Thailand, the bars and the girls and how to treat the Thai people respectfully. To be honest, I did not find out until being in Thailand for several days, but a lot of the guy's advice was fantasy rather than fact. We arrived in

Bangkok and made our way to our hotel which was located near to Khao San Road. I don't think anyone will ever forget that first feeling of walking out of the heavily air-conditioned airport in Bangkok and into an almost furnace of heat, humidity and pollution, still we had arrived in Bangkok. Like any other newbie's we made some mistakes, firstly being talked into booking an expensive airport limo, live and learn.

After reaching the hotel we get showered, changed and headed off to the famous Khao San Road. The feeling was like no other, the sounds and the smells of the street food. Even though one of the group had been to Thailand before as I mentioned earlier in the story, we fell for the old tuk tuk scam to the ping pong shows…that was mistake number two. I've heard many nightmare stories about those venues about people getting ripped off for thousands of baht, but we actually had a great time and never got bothered once while we were there.

Our first three days in Bangkok were really good, both the daytime and of course the nights, where we went out partying! In the day we went out visiting the temples and doing all the touristy things you do in a new city. On our last night in Bangkok, we decided to go for a nice meal in a restaurant near our hotel on Rambuttri, I'm sure a lot of your listeners and readers will know the one right at the start of the street that is all lit with the Thai style lanterns outside. We sat down for dinner where we were met by a beautiful Thai serving girl who looked no older than eighteen but was actually about twenty-seven. We continued to enjoy our evening with lots of food and lots of Chang beer! All four of us were flirting with the Thai girl that worked there and asked her to join us for the night when she had finished work. She accepted and we hit Khao San Road for the third and final night in Bangkok.

It was the usual crazy night with lots of Chang beer and lots of Thai food. The night finely came to an end, and I found myself with the beautiful Thai girl in some random hotel lobby drinking beer while she was eating Thai food. We ended up getting a room in this hotel as I was sharing a room back at my hotel and wanted some privacy for the upcoming gymnastics. We had a great evening and she never asked me for anything which I thought was great. If this is Thailand, I can live with it; not spending too much money was not to last however! Many thousands of baht have exchanged hands since then. I guess I got lucky and being much younger than today, I properly looked a bit more appealing to the girls than I do currently.

We left for Koh Samui the following afternoon, but before we left, I popped into the restaurant and exchanged Facebook contact details with my new girlfriend from last night. We visited Koh Samui, Phuket and Phi Phi Island. We joined in all of the full moon and half-moon parties; it was great fun back then. I wouldn't dream of doing that stuff now but being eleven years ago it was all fun to me.

After four weeks of what had been the absolute best time of my life, meeting and making friends with lots of people and some who I still keep in contact with today, it was time to fly on to Australia.

We landed in Sydney, and I was feeling very sad at leaving Thailand. There I was in an amazing city like Sydney and all I wanted to do is get back on a flight straight back to Bangkok! Nonetheless, I went with the flow of the group and continued to enjoy my time in Australia. We spent three weeks in Sydney enjoying Christmas and New Year on Darling Harbour. We then rented a campervan and drove to Melbourne, driving along the coast, stopping of at a number of places to spend the night. We all enjoyed the beautiful southeast coastline of Australia. My funds were getting very low at this point and as I arrived in Melbourne and after paying for a week's rent in a hostel my funds had finally run out!

I went to an Internet cafe across the road as smart phones weren't around that much back then. I searched online for a job and luckily started work the next morning, the job scene was much better back then. I was enjoying my time in Australia, but I could not get Thailand out my mind. I just wanted to be back there. The Australian girls are stunning, but I am not the most handsome man on the planet, so I never really stood a chance of getting together with a beautiful Australian girl. Around this time most of our group of guys from Nottingham had agreed to split up and go their separate ways.

After a few months of installing loft insulation in Melbourne and earning a very good salary, I had managed to save a little money and was planning another camping trip up to Darwin. It was a huge shock to the system coming from

Thailand where £20 can go a long way if you're careful. Compared to Australia where it is very expensive for everything! Me and another guy headed up to Darwin again stopping off and camping along the way. We had another amazing time experiencing the Australian outback with all its wildlife, totally different to England and all the time never forgetting about Thailand and constantly talking about Bangkok at every opportunity that I could.

Again, I was getting very low on funds, so I started looking for another job. Someone mentioned a couple of Pearl boat companies in Darwin but had said you don't stand much chance of getting a job with them as every backpacker in town is after the same job.

Nonetheless me and one of the other guys tried our luck and headed off to the office of the Pearl boat company. We walked in and the guy at the desk asked what we wanted?

"A job," we replied.

It was then that the phone rang and the guy at the desk answered. He continued to have a conversation with the man on the other end of the phone and just before he hung up, he asked if they were going to replace the two backpackers that had recently been sacked for stealing pearls?

He put the phone down and said,

"This is your lucky day boys, when can you start?"

This job was just what I was looking for. six weeks on, three weeks off, and on my three weeks off I was going to fly back to Thailand. This job wasn't just ideal for me to get back to Thailand it was one the best experiences of my life. Working in the Northern Territory on a boat in shark infested waters the wildlife was unbelievable!

So, the first break I got I sailed back to Darwin and booked the first flight to Phuket via Singapore. I had to spend the night in Singapore, which I didn't mind at all, as it's a beautiful city with also lots of fun things to do.

Whilst working on the boat I made friends with a really cool German guy named Marcel. I introduced him to Thailand for the first time and we returned on every break we had. After a year of being away I returned to the UK.

I started back at work in the UK and saved up to go back and travel some more. I was always interested in going back to tour Vietnam, Laos and Cambodia. So, after a few months saving up I flew back to Bangkok and had some more trips planned in Southeast Asia. Vietnam and Laos were great fun, but I couldn't wait to get back to Thailand.

The Thai girl I told you about earlier in the story who we had met in the restaurant had now moved to Phuket and opened her own little travel shop. You know the type that you see all over Thailand for booking your trips to the islands, bus, boat and train tickets and so on. We had kept in touch all this time on messenger, and she offered me a job working in her travel shop.

I was interested in staying in Thailand for a longer period of time and thought this could be a good opportunity to do that. I made my way to Phuket by bus as I was again getting a little low on funds.

After finding an apartment and paying a month's rent near the travel shop, I was literally broke. I wasn't really worried about this as I was making a little bit of money at the travel shop, just enough to eat and drink. It wasn't about partying at this point it was just about staying in Thailand and living the Thai lifestyle. I was probably the poorest farang in Thailand at this point, but I didn't care as it was just great to be there and wake up every morning in the country I loved so much. I was also waiting for a tax return that was being processed from my time working in Australia so I knew eventually I would receive around £1500 transferred to my UK bank account.

I was living on around 200 to 300 baht per day but having the best time of my life. I didn't really enjoy working in the travel shop as the Thai girl I was working for didn't really have the same happy go lucky attitude she had when we first met in Bangkok, in fact she had turned into a real misery and wasn't pleasant to work for.

After finishing work one day I decided to have a walk down Bangla Road and see if I could find some kind of other job. Most of the bar owners laughed at me when I asked them for work, but I continued to try. I decided to turn up a Soi off Bangla Road called Soi Sea Dragon, I'm sure a lot of your listeners and readers will know the street. I walked slowly up the Soi just looking for a friendly faced bar owner to approach when I came to a bar called Coney Bar. The bar was covered with balloons with food laid out as it was one of the bar girl's birthday.

The owner of the bar invited me to sit down and eat so I did and ordered a drink.

The owner came and sat with me and asked all the usual questions,

"What is your name and what do I have planned for the night."

"I'm looking for a job." I replied.

Looking at me a little confused,

"A job? But you are farang, why you want job?"

After explaining my situation to her she said,

"You're serious, aren't you? I try to help you, wait one minute."

I carried on drinking my beer not expecting anything spectacular to develop, when the lady returned with an Asian guy. I first thought he was Thai but after speaking with him he told me he was Malaysian and owned four Go-Go bars in Soi Sea Dragon and was looking for an English-speaking manager. I told him I would be interested, and so began to follow him inside one of his Go-Go bars. We walked inside and as you would expect, around twenty scantily clad girls where dancing on stage. I thought all my Christmas's had come at once. He showed me around a little and said you can start tonight if you like. I worked there for around three months all in all and it was an awesome experience. I was still very new to Thailand at this point, but this job taught me a lot about what goes on with the girls and how they have numerous farangs sending them cash.

I literally witnessed every scenario with these girls in the time I spent there, but I had lots of fun and all the girls made me feel very welcome. I actually still keep in touch with a couple of them to this day. My salary was laughable if I'm honest, just 9000 baht a month but I wasn't there for the money it was all about the experience. As soon as the tax rebate I spoke of earlier in the story was debited into my account I finished the job and enjoyed around 3 weeks holiday and of course I went on to spend time with my favourite girl I had been watching for the last 3 months but had been off limits to me as I worked in the Go-Go bar.

Since 2009 and my first time leaving Europe, I have been all around the world and would say travel is by far my biggest passion. I have plans to go to many more countries and want to experience many more adventures, but Thailand will always be my go-to place. After all the countries I have visited, Thailand is by far my favourite country! No disrespect to any other country but Thailand is just something else. I also introduced Thailand to my father as a 60-year-old and let's just say after endless amounts of advice before his first trip he made every rookie mistake in the book but that's another story. Thank you so much and I will continue to watch your channel every week. Hopefully we will meet someday in Thailand and enjoy a beer when we can all get back there.

****

Story 13.

From a Woman

I arrived on one of the small Islands in Thailand in 2004 from England (via Australia, South Pacific and New Zealand). I am dual British and American and had lived all my life in England but at the age of thirty-five, I was having a bit of a mid-life crisis.

I landed a job in one of the diving operations managed by a German woman in her early to mid-thirties named Emilia. She had been in Thailand for a few years after a career in Germany working as a teacher and then, like many, got bored and wanted to try something new out in a faraway place.

After only a few days working here, I noticed that Emilia had a rather hands-on way of working with her male staff - both farang and Thai. That would have been considered unprofessional and inappropriate in most western workplaces.

One evening after several vodka and Red Bulls, Emilia confided in me that she was terribly infatuated with a young Thai man who had done some work for her on the boat. One huge problem; this boy happened to be the fiancée of a Thai woman whose family was fairly well-connected on the island. I tried to warn her, dissuade her from continuing this because only bad things can come from these sorts of indiscretions. Not too long before this, a Dutch woman had to flee the island on a night ferry after hiding out in the bushes because she'd upset a jealous local with similar sexual indiscretions. Emilia had thrown caution to the wind and was convinced nothing bad was going to happen.

Some farangs were convinced they were invincible or untouchable because they felt their foreign status would protect them and others had the attitude that if you didn't acknowledge a problem, then the said problem didn't exist.

Several months went by and Emilia's business was struggling - due to the combination of low season with particularly bad weather, her lack of business knowledge and her continuing hang-ups with the men in her surroundings. Fortunately, the object of her biggest affection, the Thai man's promise to the wealthy businesswoman, moved away to Bangkok. During my various stints on the island, I met an array of foreign women all with their reasons for being there. You had the young women exploring life and places on their gap years or post-university partiers; the mid-life crisis brigade; the Shirley Valentine divorcees; old and jaded women fed up with careers, with men in their life and with their existence. The biggest basket-case of a woman I knew during my time was the owner of the dive shop managed by Emilia. Charlotte was an English woman in her mid-thirties, well-educated, articulate and I imagine, she would be considered interesting and attractive (average height and weight, neither spectacular nor ugly looking). Since aged eighteen, Charlotte had suffered from a strong desire to travel, and she had worked and lived in far-flung places. She had some training in nursing so that enabled her to find work to subsidise her misadventures in remote developing regions where such services were sadly lacking.

Charlotte also had parents with business interests in Thailand, so she always had something to fall back on when she messed up. Charlotte was also a heavy drinker and had the tendency to tell stories of her adventures under the influence, I had gotten cornered into hearing many of these at our usual beach bar hangout. She had a taste for exotic men and a rather odd maternal complex combined with a dubious white saviour mindset. So, I figured that in less than fifteen years, Charlotte had lived and worked in: Spain, Egypt, Western Samoa, The Cooks, Solomon Islands, Papua New Guinea and a few others before arriving in Thailand around the turn of the century. In Samoa, she had an adulterous affair with the son of some village chief, and she had to leave in a hurry. In Papua New Guinea, she was in a passionate relationship with a young man and found herself pregnant. She would show her colleagues and friends photos of herself happily posing with a pregnant bump with the then love of her life. But beyond this, nobody really knew what had happened because depending on who she was talking to, she would say she either: A) realised things were not working out in this relationship and had an abortion;

or B) Her lover's family would not accept a white woman as part of their family and kicked her out and forced her to leave her child behind; or C) Had a difficult and life-threatening miscarriage late in her pregnancy. Whatever the case, I knew Charlotte was a woman with lots of baggage. Sadly, her business experience was not much better than Emilia's and this dive shop was heading for failure.

I left Thailand early 2005 and returned a year later and sure enough, the Charlotte/Emilia project had gone under, and they were blaming one another for the failure. Emilia was living in her hut with a 19-year-old Thai boy who barely spoke English. Things got rough in their relationship when Emilia's parents visited, and her teenage lover started flirting with her father – a closeted bisexual. He left shortly afterwards leaving Emilia in a real state cursing him, her father and every man she'd ever known.

Charlotte on the other hand, had managed to stay in a semi long-term arrangement with her young Thai husband named Amon, he was handsome, charming, and had a very strong work ethic and spoke a reasonable amount of English. Behind his back, Charlotte would fantasise and tell her Western friends that she had taken Amon out of the jungle and had made him what he was and had taught him everything she knew.

We all felt a bit sorry for Amon as Charlotte appeared extremely possessive, controlling and was behaving like some master imperialist. He was at her beck and call working day and night for whatever Charlotte had doing workwise. Amon's family, I was told, was proud as he was making good money and had a good standard of living - better than anyone else in his family, so he quietly worked away being his charming self.

So, when Charlotte revealed to her friends and colleagues that she was a few months pregnant in mid-2005, all we could do was smile and wish both her and Amon the best.

Despite Charlotte's pregnancy and financial stability in her businesses, her relationship with Amon was rocky to say the least. She had suspected Amon of cheating on her and was nervous. In a very unfortunate turn of events, while she was eight months pregnant, she accidentally ate a cocktail of mushrooms and prescription medication and suffered a medical emergency. As a result, she had a miscarriage and a nervous breakdown

In my final months on the island, things were a bit too strange, so I kept a healthy arms distance from the antics and dramas of others. Amon started seeing other women and for a while, he ran away off the island.

Right after the miscarriage, Charlotte found a small dog (a Maltese-type pup) and immediately, in her vulnerable state, took it as a surrogate for the child she'd lost and got extremely attached, not letting the dog out of her sight and carrying it around in a sling on her chest. I left the island in early 2007 and didn't keep in touch with Charlotte. But I did stay in touch with Emilia who stayed on the island until 2014. She was in a series of disastrous-sounding relationships with Thai men (all young, not too educated and probably needed the money). According to her, Charlotte got back together with Amon after an on-off unsteady marriage where they both cheated with others and Charlotte's dog was still with her.

****

Story 14.

Caught Red-Handed

I am from the UK and came out of a seventeen year long toxic relationship in 2019. Myself and my partner at the time had spoken of visiting Thailand but after we split up, I decided to take the plunge and take a trip to Thailand on my own.

So, at Christmas in 2019 I flew to Bangkok for what was originally meant to be a ten-day trip. I stayed in a rather lovely apartment hotel in Silom which was very cheap and discovered that I would fall in love with Thailand within twenty-four hours. As a Single man having been cheated on multiple times throughout my long relationship, I very quickly discovered the wonders that Thailand can offer a sexually active, newly single man and found myself like a kid in a sweet shop even though I was in my late forties. I had of course researched Thailand on the Internet and thought I understood what it was all about but discovered it was a hundred times better than I could ever imagine. Not just because of the beautiful women, but I fell in love with the culture, the people, the way of life, the weather of course and just about everything connected to Thailand.

Within two days I had met a sweet and gorgeous girl called Nan, and by chance bumped into three guys visiting from Scotland. These guys had been to Thailand many times and I spent the rest of my holiday hanging out with them. They taught me a lot about how everything works, the pitfalls and the delights on offer.

I spent the next few days bar-hopping and drinking more alcohol than I thought I could ever imagine doing and then my new Scottish friends told me that they were travelling down to Pattaya, which made me consider what I want to do for the rest of the holiday. While I enjoyed the company of Nan, who was now clearly more interested in one of my new friends, I didn't take it too seriously and wanted to be a free spirit and decided that I would leave her behind and travel to Pattaya with my new friends. I felt really bad telling her I was going because she was a very sweet girl and she never asked for any money...in fact she didn't have any money and I bought her drinks and food everywhere we went, but at one point she received her salary and immediately paid for my night out which I later discovered is very rare in Thailand.

When I left Bangkok, I gave her some money and let her remain in my hotel which I had checked out early to head down to Pattaya. We have since stayed in touch and she now has a boyfriend and seems happy.

I had decided to extend my stay for several days. I was spending a lot more money than I had planned on before leaving the UK. The problem being that I had now caught the Thailand bug. The Kingdom can do that, creeping up on the unsuspecting traveller. I discovered Pattaya was very different to Bangkok but for a single man, has the same kind of beer-bars and go-go bars which were brilliant and by the beach. I spent New Year's Eve in the bars and had a fantastic time for the remainder of my holiday.

I would love to say that this was the best experience of my life and I suppose it was, but it wasn't without a few bad experiences. My first bad experience was actually back in Bangkok. I was sitting in Soi 4 in the bars that are open to the street and drinking a cocktail jug that cost something like 200 Baht, a great place to people watch as it is very busy, and girls are everywhere. On the opposite side of the street there was a girl sitting who kept looking at me, but I noticed that she was with a farang, so didn't take much notice. The next thing I knew she was sitting next to me, and she started a conversation. It was obvious she wanted to have some fun, so I said,

"Shall we go to my hotel room for drinks together?"

The aerobics were great, and I went off to take a shower.

At this point it suddenly dawned on me that I was leaving myself vulnerable as my bag with my wallet and my money in it was in the room. I felt a little bit uneasy about this, so I jumped out of the shower without turning it off and immediately walked straight back into the room and as I did so, I caught her holding my wallet above my bag and just about to pull all the money out of it!

"What the hell do you think you are doing?" I raged.

Like a seasoned professional she answered,

"I am looking for your passport!"

I'm not sure how that made it any better, but she seemed to have an answer for everything. At this point I politely told her to get her stuff and leave! I then realised we were both butt naked and I suddenly felt quite vulnerable.

Anyway, she put on her clothes and disappeared, and I then realised that you have to be very careful in Thailand! After this experience I am careful to leave my bag in view of both the shower and the room!

My only other bad experience was while I was in Pattaya. One evening I decided not to crowd my new friends and spend the night on my own. I took a baht bus over to Jomtien's nightlife area to see what that was like. I met a local girl and invited her back to my hotel in Pattaya for drinks where we had fun. Afterwards I offered to pay for her taxi home and asked,

"How much would that cost."

I must admit I was quite drunk, but when she said,

"One thousand Baht." I assumed she was trying it on,

"Very funny," I said. "It's not gonna cost that much."

And that's when the problem started! She started getting quite aggressive and vocal, so I resorted to filming her as I started to think I was being the victim to some sort of scam. I tried to remain calm as I didn't want to get involved in a dispute in Thailand especially when I'm drunk and with a Thai local, especially if it was some sort of scam. So, I try to lead her outside while still recording her on my phone. her aggression got worse and then she did some sort of a flying kick at me nearly knocking me over. Considering she was considerably smaller than me it was quite worrying as I now thought,

'Crap, I'm going to end up getting arrested for violence,' even though I didn't react.

Luckily there were two Eastern European guys in the street who spoke both English and Thai and I explained my problem to them, they also listened to the girl and then pointed out to me that on the way to my hotel I didn't have change for the taxi, so she had paid for it and I had promised to pay her back.

This had completely slipped my mind and although I didn't necessarily have to pay her taxi home, this would explain why she was asking for more money than one taxi trip. As I now understood this, I decided to give her 500 Baht and that seemed to be sufficient, and she went on her way. Looking back, this was a good job because being as stubborn as I am I wouldn't have given any money since as I thought she was scamming me. I would have probably ended up in all sorts of trouble especially as I thought she was going to claim she was charging me for her company and then I didn't pay her.

It just goes to show that sometimes the best solution is to stay calm and get an alternative opinion, as being drunk can cloud your judgement!

Anyway, after two weeks I sadly had to leave Thailand, looking forward to my next visit and then of course the pandemic hit.

I've spent the last two years trying to arrange another trip to Thailand and even now I'm planning my retirement subject to a few enjoyable holidays to convince myself that is the way forward. Hopefully my next visit will be a little less problematic and as I now understand Thailand a lot better, hopefully easier to fit in. I have even started to learn the Thai language and although I'm not fluent I could certainly hold a bit of a conversation in the usual sort of tourist environments and look forward to having it tested by Thai people who can teach me more.

PETER HOPKINS

I have travelled to quite a few places in my time including Hawaii and none of them come close to the beauties and wonders that Thailand offers. I can't wait to return.

****

Story 15.

Way Back When

It was 1968, I was only nineteen years old and in the US army when I received orders to go to Thailand. I really knew very little about Thailand other than it was in Southeast Asia and it was not Vietnam and for that, I felt that I was very fortunate. I arrived in Thailand via the Don Muang airport. At that time, the Don Muang airport was the main airport in Thailand.

The following day I was on an army bus heading to Korat. The road to Korat was being built by the US Army with the help of local workers. There were several sections of the highway that were still a dirt/mud road. The very next day, I was in the back of an army jeep heading south to a small army base that was being built about two kilometers west of the U Tapao air base. This is the same U Tapao that is now an international airport but in 1968 it

was a military air base where the B52
bombers were stationed. Most of the GIs
on the base listened to a military radio
station that broadcast out of the U Tapao
base. It played typical 1960s rock and roll
music.

Within a day or two, I noticed that four
or five times a day the DJ would play a
song like, "Will you still love me
tomorrow?" Then read off a series of
numbers…4, 28, 63, 67, etc. I kept
thinking,

'What's up with the numbers? Is it
some kind of lottery? And if so, how do I
buy some tickets? Is it coordinates being
broadcast for the B52s on their bombing
runs?'

So, I asked one of the other GIs what's
up with the numbers?

He said, "Have you been downtown
yet?"

I said that I had just arrived in the
country less than a week ago and really
had not had much time to get downtown.

He said, "This Saturday some of us are
going into town, come with us and we
will show you about the numbers."

We typically worked five and a half
days a week. We would have Saturday
afternoon off and all-day Sunday. Well,
Saturday arrived and four or five of us

went into town. There were maybe a dozen bars, a couple were listed as being off limits to military personnel. There were also several jewellery stores where you could buy souvenirs of Thailand. There were a few restaurants and a couple of tailor shops.

We went into a bar and ordered a round of Singha beers. Oh My Gosh, there were maybe a dozen gorgeous ladies in the bar. A few of them came over to our table. I never regarded myself as really good looking but these gorgeous young ladies all thought that I was a very handsome man. One of the ladies sat down next to me and began talking to me. She wanted to know if I had a girlfriend in Thailand. When I told her that I had just got into the country, she informed me that she could be my girlfriend.

One of the other GIs pointed out to me that each lady wore a button with a number.

He said, "OK, the lady that you are talking to has a button with the number fifty-seven on it. Each lady is tested once a week by the air force medics, and it was not MOVID that they were being tested for." He continued, "If she tests positive, she is given a shot of penicillin, she cannot work for a week or two and her number is read on the radio the following week. So, if you take number fifty-seven to a hotel tonight and her number is read on the radio next week, you should consider going on sick call to be tested. If a bar refuses to have their ladies tested, that bar is put off limits."

I thought, 'what were the words from the movie, the Wizard of Oz? Something tells me we are not in Kansas anymore.'

Within several weeks, I became good friends with another GI. His name was John. To this date, I refer to him as my army brother. The two of us became friends with a local guy named Kittibun. He worked on the base. Kittibun lived in a small village about three or four kilometers from camp. He would frequently invite us to his "Thai-house," then John and I finally took him up on the offer. Kittibun's Thai-house was a small one room plywood shack. There was a light, a fan, and a bed for sleeping. There also was no indoor plumbing. The first time I saw his Thai-house, I was shocked that this was his home. However, after a few more visits, his Thai-house began to grow on me. It soon became our home away from home. We would go to his house, maybe sit on the floor, have some food and then head over to the local pool hall for a game of snooker. There was also a fresh fruit stand in the village. I would typically pick up some fruit to take back to camp.

In 1968, Pattaya was a small fishing village with a few bars and an excellent beach. It was maybe twenty-five or thirty kilometres north of where we were stationed. As I mentioned previously, we would typically have Saturday afternoon and all-day Sunday off. John and I made numerous visits to Pattaya. You could take a taxi but that would cost you maybe forty or fifty baht. I do not know for sure because we never took the taxi. Being privates in the army, we did not make a lot of money and so we became a couple of cheap Charlies. We would go out to the Sukhumvit highway and wait for the large bus that was heading to Bangkok. They ran approximately every thirty minutes. We would flag down the bus, pay five Baht and forty-five minutes later we would be at a gravel road that led down into Pattaya. The bus did not go into Pattaya but stayed on the Sukhumvit highway heading north to Bangkok. The bus could actually stop at two locations to get to Pattaya. I have no idea of exactly where these roads were, but I suspect that they are now the Pattaya South and the

Pattaya North roads. We would typically get off at the south road. Occasionally there would be a taxicab or baht bus sitting there waiting for a customer. If there was, we would take it down to the beach road. If not, we would walk. It was maybe a kilometre to the beach. The walk made that first beer taste that much better.

There was a hand full of bars in Pattaya, a snack bar, and one or two hotels. There was no Walking Street, however one of the bars that we would frequent was in the area of Walking Street. It was one of the few buildings on the beach side of Beach Road. I think its name was something like Friends Bar or Friendship Bar. Several of the ladies that worked at the bar lived in rooms above the bar. There was another bar that we would frequent, I am not sure of the name, but it was owned by a local named Kob. We always referred to it as Kob's Place. There was also an upscale bar connected to the Nippa Lodge, which was the highest hotel in Pattaya back then. Someone was renting motor bikes. You could rent a bike and drive up to Buddha Hill or just cruise up and down beach road. There were also a few boys that would rent you a large inner tube for a half day, that you could use as a raft for floating on the water. For several months I rented a small apartment with no indoor plumbing in Pattaya for 100 Baht a month.

Whenever I hear a song by the Beach Boys, it takes me back to when I was a young kid chilling out in Pattaya, Thailand.

Occasionally we would get a three-day pass. When we did, we were on our way to Bangkok. As with Pattaya, you could take a taxi to Bangkok however it would cost maybe 150 or 200 Baht. But that same bus that took us to Pattaya would continue on to Bangkok. It cost 15 Baht and three hours later you would be pulling into the Ekkamai bus station in Bangkok.

The Ekkamai bus station still exists. If you are on the sky train today and are at the Nana Station, the next stop is Asok. Three or four more stops heading south, and you are at Ekkamai.

Bangkok in 1968-1969 was a bit different than Bangkok 2022. There was no sky train, no subway, or overhead highways. There were also no high-rise buildings, no KFC, and believe it or not, no 7-11's. There were local buses. They cost 50 satang (100 satang = 1 Baht). We would use the local Bangkok busses to navigate around the city. Most of the bars from 1969 have long since gone out of business. About the only one that I am aware of that is still there is The Thermae Coffee shop. The Thermae is currently near Soi 13 on Sukhumvit. I do not remember where it was located back in 1969. There were several GI hotels along Sukhumvit and the New Phetchaburi Road. They were all very similar. They were maybe five or six stories high and were air conditioned. They typically had an outdoor swimming pool. And they had indoor plumbing, and that was a treat. The price was typically 120 Baht per night if you were a GI coming from Vietnam. However, if you could speak Thai, you could get a room for 80 Baht per night. There was a Mexican restaurant on Sukhumvit around Soi 25. I think that it was called the Nipa Hut. It was a great place for tacos.

On several occasions, John and I would get a massage. On one occasion we were getting massages in adjacent rooms. About halfway through the massage, John was not exactly pleased with his massage. He called to me through the paper-thin walls and asked if I was still there? At the time I was butt naked, face down on the table and this young lady is walking on my back. Even though she weighed maybe forty-five or fifty kilos, it was kind of restricting my breathing. I struggled to answer that I was still there. I am not sure what he thought was happening in my room, owing to the fact that I struggled with answering him. He then asked me how my massage was going. I started to answer that it was going well, but the young lady did not like me talking to the guy in the adjacent room. She pressed her heal into my back and said,

"You no speak to him. If you want to speak, you speak to me."

I wanted to say, "Yes ma'am, whatever you say," but I could hardly breathe to talk.

Then I thought, 'Okay, if she asks me how many B52s are at U Tapao, only give her your name, rank and serial number.'

As it turns out I really did enjoy the massage, but I never went back to that establishment for another massage.

In March 1969, Kittibun said that a special Thai festival, Songkran, was coming up in April. If we could get a short leave, we could go to Chang Mai for the festival. To get to Chang Mai, we would take a train from the Hua Lampong station in Bangkok. It took seventeen hours to reach Chang Mai. John and I were the only non-Thai people on the train, it felt like something out of a Hemingway novel. The train was third world. There were wooden benches for seats. The windows slid down into the sides of the railway cars. Occasionally someone might board the train carrying a cage with two or three live chickens in it. At train stops, locals would board the train and try to sell a variety of foods.

Kittibun eventually became a Buddha monk, not that he was super religious, it was a way to avoid the Thai draft. John and I were invited to his village up country for the ceremony. The village was in the north. It was very rural, and the roads only extended out to a few of the surrounding villages. For most of the locals, we were the first Americans that they had seen. There was no indoor plumbing anywhere in the village. To take a bath, you would put on a sarong and head down to the river where you would remove the sarong and wade into the river and wash yourself. I think that half the village turned out to watch the two Americans giving themselves a bath. We were just glad that nobody in the village owned a movie camera or a regular camera. I spent two years in

Thailand. While there, there were a couple of young ladies that touched my heart, but being so young and not sure where my life would lead once I left Thailand. The thought of marriage did not enter my mind. As it turns out, a couple years after returning to the USA, I met the love of my life. We were married for forty-seven years before she died of an ongoing lung issue.

In January 2020, I met up with John in Bangkok for a mini reunion. My how things had changed. We returned to the States just days before Thailand went into lockdown for the pandemic

If Thailand fully reopens, I would like to go back, maybe for an extended period of time. I suspect that this might be early 2023. While there, I would like to go up to the village where Kittibun was originally from and see if there is anyone that remembers him or his family. I suspect that there are family members who still live in the area.

One of the things that I would like to do is to find him and tell him what a good friend he was to a young kid that was 10,000 miles from home.

****

Story 16.

Marrying a freelancer

As a recent subscriber to your channel, I have listened to quite a few of your viewers stories with great interest. I would like to tell you about my own experience. It was after a three-year relationship breakup in the UK with a British woman, that I was encouraged by some friends to go on holiday to Thailand as a way of forgetting my bitter breakup and experience the delights of the city of Pattaya.

Upon arriving in Pattaya in the winter of 2017 with a couple of my friends for a four-week holiday, they showed me how things worked in Pattaya and especially everything about the night life.

Being my first time in Thailand I was warned by my friends,

"Do not fall in love with a bar girl, especially in Pattaya."

On my first night I was taken to the bright lights of Walking Street, Pattaya and ended up in a notorious freelancer bar where the women outnumber the men by, it must be at least three to one. I was let loose in what I can only describe as a shop full of sweets and not deciding which one to pick first!

Having never experienced women staring at you and giving the come on so readily was really a strange experience. However, one of my friends came to my rescue and suggested,

"Why not look around and just pick the prettiest one in the bar."

Taking his suggestion and after scanning around I decided to approach what I can only describe as the most beautiful slim, dark-skinned girl, a typical Asian looking woman with long dark hair that covered her face and with the most gorgeous smile and full set of perfect teeth with a diamond in her tooth that shone brightly as she smiled. After a few drinks and dancing she came with me to my hotel room for some more drinks. Her English wasn't great but OK, and we used Google translate for the difficult words. We got on really well. After a few more drinks and some nighttime swimming in the pool we were both exhausted. My *beautiful* new friend stayed with me overnight, but it was only to sleep and nothing else, as said we were both very, very tired.

Waking in the morning to find this beautiful woman lying next to me was like I had gone to heaven and woke up with an angel next to me, I know that sounds corny, but I was older than her so felt lucky. Anyway, I compensated her for her time, we said our goodbyes and she left with a smile on her face. For the following week or so we were out every night, drinking and partying. Being older I had to admit to myself that I could not keep up at this pace and would have to slow it down a bit. So, I thought the second week, I would try to meet a woman that I could stay longer with and maybe do a few tourist trips with as I still had 3 weeks left of my holiday.

One of my new Thai friends introduced me to a nice-looking woman. A pretty girl who would take me out each day on the back of her motorcycle and we enjoyed the local sights such as temples, beaches, and we ate lots of nice meals together. I felt a little uncomfortable when out and about with this girl as I was quite a bit older than her which I guess is normal for Pattaya but was strange for me.

At the start of my third week, I decided to meet up with my friends and re-visit the freelancer bar on Walking Street that I had visited on my first night. As soon as we arrived, I noticed the drop-dead gorgeous lady that I had met and took back to my hotel on the first night in Pattaya. After an hour or so I noticed she had not coupled up with anyone and I watched as she seemed to ignore the attentions of other men who approached her. I approached her and apologised for the last time we had met for getting so drunk. She laughed and said it was ok. We then started to chat and again we got on just great, dancing and drinking we ended up back at my hotel room for more drinks once again. I got on so much better with this girl than the girl who had been picking me up on her scooter each day so decided to come clean and tell her that I was not going to meet her again as I much preferred the company of this girl.

I asked this gorgeous girl if she would like to remain with me for the rest of my holiday and of course I would compensate her for her time. I soon realised that this girl was after as much as she could get out of me and when I asked her,

"Do you even like me?"

She said, "NO, I only like your money."

I asked her to leave.

She kept turning up at my hotel and knocking my door, did she think that I was some kind of an idiot? Well, I'm not.

In my short time in Pattaya I had learned from friends how the bargirls generally take you for what they can get. One friend told me how he was with his girlfriend for over two years and was planning to get married, after giving her £20,000 to set up home, she had disappeared. Another friend told me how his girlfriend managed to get £5,000 out of him before she also disappeared. I thought I was not going to get caught out like this, famous last words, right? Nevertheless, My Thai girlfriend named Jitt, soon stopped asking me for extra money when I told her I did not have too much money left.

Jitt still stayed with me for the duration of my holiday which lasted for four weeks. During the two weeks with her I must admit it was the best time of my life, partying, dancing, eating out and visiting local tourist sites, this lady made me feel and act young again and I was a typical tourist, two-week millionaire in her eyes.

At the end of the four-week holiday I got to know her reasonably well and I thought we became close… I said I would keep in touch when I got home, and perhaps help her out even though I knew she was a working, if you get my meaning. Arriving back home to the UK, I kept in touch with Jitt via messenger and we talked on live stream almost every day. Jitt said she missed me and asked when I would see her again. Considering it was now winter 2018 in the UK and it was freezing, I made the decision to go back to Pattaya at the end of the month and meet up with Jitt again… but only if she considered going back home to her village to wait for me.

Jitt's home was in Khon Kaen in the North of Thailand, which is in a province called Isaan. As long as I paid for her journey and gave her a little money to live on, she agreed to wait for me. Being skeptical I really thought she wouldn't accept my offer. Talking to Jitt almost every day whilst she was home in her village, took away any doubts and worries that she was working back in Pattaya. After arranging my visa for a three month stay, I booked my return ticket at the end of the month and asked Jitt to meet me at the airport.

Arriving at Bangkok airport Mid-February 2018 I had arranged for her to meet me at my gate exit. I had waited for three hours at our agreed meeting point at the airport, and I thought I had been stood-up, only for Jitt to arrive holding a huge bunch of flowers and the biggest smile I had ever seen. Jitt told me that she had been waiting at the wrong place. Perhaps this was because of our language barrier so I gave her the benefit of the doubt and hoped that she had not simply come straight from Pattaya in a taxi.

The following three months went so quickly, and we enjoyed each other's company. I had no intentions of falling in love, I just wanted a holiday girlfriend, as I had just reached my retirement age of sixty-five. I have been married twice and after fathering a couple of children, I felt that I had done my bit for humanity. During this holiday we had a fantastic time in Pattaya, we also travelled North and visited Jitt's parents in her village. Meeting her family and friends it became very clear to me why some girls would want to head to the bright lights of Pattaya to earn a decent living. Her family are dirt poor and have very little, I truly felt sorry for them. Their only income comes from long hours of toil working in the paddy fields. Working in the bars was perhaps their only salvation and a glimmer of a better life, hoping they would meet their white knight in shining armour. In a way I feel sorry for the countless thousands of women who have to work in Pattaya and in the bar business just to feed their families, and a lot of the time a young child or several children that were abandoned by the father back the villages.

Perhaps it was because of this that I decided to rescue this beautiful lady from a life of freelancing in Pattaya. I was met by many skeptical friends who all said Jitt would take me for my money, and I was just one of many others who sent her money as soon as I was back in the UK and the list goes on from all my so-called friends. All I knew is that I was very lucky to find such a caring Thai woman who was so beautiful that men turned their heads as she walked by. For those who are lucky enough to find a Thai girl, they will soon discover that they look after their man far better than any Western women would want to. Again, arriving back home to the UK we kept in touch on a daily basis. I would speak to Jitt using a live stream podcast, that way I knew she did not go back to her old life.

It was difficult for a while, but I persuaded Jitt to come to the UK on a tourist visa, just to see if perhaps one day she may like to come and live with me. After a few complications trying to sort things out which I couldn't, in the end I used a company based in Thailand to help sort out the visa. It cost me about £500 but was worth every penny. The main problem I faced when Jitt arrived in the UK was customs at the airport, as an over-zealous customs officer would not believe her reason for visiting the UK and thought the worst. I am guessing mainly because of her lack of English. After a three-hour delay, they finely let her into the country after she persuaded the customs officer to phone me via her internet messenger to prove she was visiting a real person. Perhaps it was my fault as I had arranged a four-month holiday for her, but her visa stated three months, but in the end, we were finally together once again.

The next four months was again perhaps the next best time of my life. I showed Jitt the lifestyle of the Western world to the envy of my jealous friends. The funniest moment being one day after a snow fall. We would walk in the park, and she found it amusing that she could throw snowballs at strangers as they walked past and wouldn't say a word, they just smiled. Jitt said she saw this in the movies. I had to explain we don't normally do things like this in real life, but we had some great fun together. It was during her stay that my gorgeous Thai girlfriend became pregnant, telling me that it was the best thing to ever happen in her life and how she wanted a daughter so badly that one day her daughter would look after her in her old age, just as she had done for her parents for so many years. I suppose it's a tradition that we in the Western world can't appreciate. It was heart breaking knowing my beautiful Thai girlfriend was going back to her own country, even though I tried to persuade her to stay in the UK, explaining that our child would have a better life here away from the poverty of her village. But she felt a duty to her parents to go back and have our child in her own country.

During the next eight months we kept in touch as usual and I watched her blossom with her pregnancy, her parents were there to help. During this time apart I needed to go back into employment so that I could save enough money to go back for the birth of our child. Being on a pension was hard enough anyway. Soon the eight months was over, I was on the first plane back to Thailand to be present at the birth. It was now fast approaching the end of 2019.

After a long night of labour in November, our daughter was born and I must say, that having experienced hospitals in the UK and in Thailand I know which give a better personal service. Sorry to say this but we could learn a lot from the Thai's.

Shortly after the birth we decided to get married, so our daughter had my name and possible British Citizenship. Travelling to Bangkok to the British embassy on my own from the North was an experience and that was just to apply for the marriage certificate.

Upon my return we got married in the local temple in Khon Kaen. It was a quiet affair with just myself, Jitt and our baby present. It was almost clinical and formal affair with just a couple of forms to sign and producing our ID's, that was it, we were married. We planned to have a village party someday in the future to celebrate, where I would offer a dowry to my new mother and father in-laws. It was now January 2020 and sadly my three-month visa was about to expire, and I had to return to the UK, having only experienced the joy of our baby daughter for less than a month. Due to the 90-day visa and the 31 days in a month I was over my period of stay and was fined at the airport upon my exit. I was planning to go back later in the year to see Jitt and our daughter, but the dreaded pandemic struck and due to travel restrictions, I was trapped in the UK.

Watching our baby grow from afar is devastating, we talk every day, and I can see the bond between mother and daughter grow. My biggest regret is not being there with them both. It is now June 2021 and I hope to return when restrictions have ended, hopefully by the end of the year I will be with them again. Our daughter will be two years old by the time I get back to Thailand. I regret not being there in Thailand as my daughter is growing up. This Worldwide pandemic has a lot to answer for, but one thing is certain, I will make it up to them when I can eventually return. The reason why I share my story is to show that not all bargirls or freelancers are out to get what they can and that there are some genuine women who would dearly love to meet their knight in shining armour and given the time and patience, love can conquer all barriers. In the meantime, there is a wedding party to organize.

****

Story 17.

The Jealous 'Girlfriend'

This is an instruction manual on what NOT to do on a trip to Pattaya! Viewers and readers will cringe when they hear what I did!

I was going through a divorce and so desperately needed some R&R. I had been to Pattaya once before with a previous Thai Girlfriend I met in Australia. The Thai girlfriend and I split up, or so I thought! (More on this later).

So, I thought to myself 'divorce nearly done, Thai girlfriend gone. Time to go to Pattaya and have a good time!'

A nine-hour flight from Sydney, Australia and here I was in Bangkok.

First mistake, don't get a pink or yellow & green taxi to Pattaya downstairs on the first floor. I was approached by several touts but managed to ward them off as they asked for 3,000 Baht for the trip. Lucky for me a Pattaya regular took pity on me and said,

"Get a taxi downstairs."

To which the tout replied,

"Ok, I will take you to Pattaya for 2000 Baht."

I confirmed again with him that was all I would pay is 2000 Baht and he agreed.

We then walked to the multi-story car park. I knew something wasn't right, but my fears were relieved somewhat when a gleaming new minivan pulled up being driven by a beautiful Thai girl who could speak perfect English. (Another warning sign missed. I should have run then and there).

I got in the van and thought, 'things are looking up.' I couldn't believe my luck!

Then a few minutes later her mobile started ringing and her English changed to Thai. All of a sudden, I am being told,

"Pattaya long way, you need to change car"

The van then starts heading down all these side streets into a grubby part of town.

'Oh no,' I thought. 'How could I have been so naive? Now I am going to get robbed and wake up with one less kidney!'

Then the van pulled into a car park full of dodgy looking cars driven by equally dodgy looking characters. I was told to get out of the van and go in a clapped-out old Volvo with some Indian guy. I protested but was quickly surrounded by a lot of these characters and I thought that I had better shut up now!

Then the Thai cutie says, "You have to pay 800 extra."

"No, I don't! The guy told me two thousand. Call him and check" I replied.

She apparently calls him and then says, "No, he said you have to pay two thousand eight hundred."

I protest again as I realise I am being ripped off and then she says,

"You have to pay eight hundred, or I have to pay him eight hundred."

Stupid me, completely naive again feels sorry for the girl, so I pay the 800 Baht, what an idiot! I can't believe that I was so stupid and was conned so easily.

This was only my third visit to Thailand. We have all made the same mistakes, I am sure. But my ordeal doesn't end there. I still have two more occasions to be ripped off yet!

Finally, the car starts to move, and boy am I glad to finally get out from that place. The drive to Pattaya is uneventful except the driver takes back roads that I have never seen before and comes into Pattaya from the back.

'Where's the beach?' I think.

Then my heart starts racing again, I am going to be robbed... another kidney, etc. So, I start to freak out remembering all the stories from Banged Up Abroad. A TV series from back home. I tell the guy to stop the car - NOW! He does and as luck would have it, right outside the VC hotel (not far from Walking St). Silly me of course doesn't realise that I am so close to Beach Road that I should have been able to smell the cheap perfume from there and I wonder,

'Where the hell am I?'

The driver says that he will get a good price for me at the hotel. (Conned again - come in spinner!) I accept the deal as I just want to get out of the car, but needless to say I have probably just paid for his kids last three years at high school with this deal! I check into my room... not bad,

"Would sir like to upgrade for an extra 300 Baht?"

"Yes, sir would."

Conned again! (That probably paid for his kid's dental work too!)

I go for a walk and finally manage to find Beach Road - things are improving. Walking along minding my own business this beautiful girl starts smiling at me.

"What are you doing?" I ask.

"Waiting for you" she replies! "I go with you?"

"Go where?" I asked stupidly, not believing my luck.

"Your room. Can drink together."

After a bit more small talk, we went back to my hotel for drinks. Once again being so naive I couldn't find my way back to the hotel. After hopping on two-baht buses (those pickup trucks with the two rows of seats that you hop on and off for 10 Baht a trip.), completely frustrated by this time, I just end up getting a taxi and paying 100 Baht and of course no meter, ripped off again! But I didn't care as I just wanted some nice female company. No stopping at the front desk to pay a joiner fee or show her ID card, lucky for me this girl was legit, or I would have been in trouble again. I was later to find out that paying the joiner fee is a good investment as protection for both you and the girl. She is watched over by hotel staff in case you are some kind of nut job who wants to hurt her. Anyway, she was great company and we ended up getting drunk together in my room.

I called the girl a number of times and we met up and had fun together around the bars.

My new Beach Road girlfriend asks, "How come you know some Thai?"

I told her that I used to have a Thai girlfriend in Australia.

"No problem," she says. "I be your girlfriend now"

I thought to myself, 'Thank you to my ex-wife for the divorce!'

But all good things must come to an end and reluctantly I had to head back to Sydney and finalise the divorce and the usual mundane exercise of going to work to make money and pay it to the ex-wife. On arrival in Sydney my ex-Thai girlfriend calls,

"Where are you? I need to see you."

"But aren't we broken up?" I asked.

"No," she says. "Why would you think that?"

I said "No reason. It's just that we haven't seen each other for months after our disagreement and you moved out"

Anyway, as I still liked her, I was happy to get back with her. A few days later, she drove from where she lived in the country to my house to, "surprise me," when I came home from work, as she still had a key. She surprised me alright! She decided to unpack my bag from Thailand, and wouldn't you know it she found 'Beach Road girlfriend's' number!

Of course, she rang it! "Hello, who are you?"

Beach Road girlfriend says, "I am Ross's girlfriend."

Real Thai girlfriend says, "But hasn't he got a Thai girlfriend in Australia?"

"No, that girl not good lady. I am girlfriend now," says Beach Road girlfriend!

I had no idea this was going on till I get a call from my 'Beach Road girlfriend'

"I just had a call from a very nice Thai lady in Australia who is going to help me be your girlfriend!"

I was mortified! I knew my Australian Thai girlfriend was incredibly jealous and I would be in for it when I got home! She yelled and screamed and made a hell of a scene.

After she cooled down, she demanded to see photos of this girl. I said there weren't any photos (but there were but thankfully I had hidden them). Then she demanded that I get a new camera, as you cannot take photos of me with the same camera that you used for the other girl!

"What photos? There aren't any photos" I said.

A few days later I thought I had better get those hidden photos and destroy them. I waited until my Australian Thai girlfriend had a shower. I looked and looked for the photos but couldn't find them - they were nowhere to be found! Girlfriend gets out of the shower and surprises me,

"What are you looking for?"

"Nothing" I say sheepishly.

Next day, same thing when girlfriend hits the shower, I start looking for the photos... sprung again!

"Looking for something?"

The gig was up so I came clean.

"Yes, the photos."

Girlfriend said, "YES, there were photos and I saw them. That girl is younger and prettier than me." So jealous! "Photos are gone, I cut them up and put them in all different bins around the street - you will never find them!"

But it didn't end there. She rang Beach Road girlfriend and said,

"Don't ever call my boyfriend again or I will come to Pattaya to see you!"

After a few weeks I thought things had calmed down... until I get out of the shower and find my Australian girlfriend on my phone to Beach Road girlfriend saying,

"How come you answer phone? I told you not to talk to my boyfriend again! I ring on his phone to see if you answer. You shouldn't answer!"

The moral of this story is... Don't EVER write down a Thai girl's number and bring it home with you! And also, don't take photos of other Thai girls unless you have a grade ten secure wall safe! The good news to this story is that I got married to the Australian Thai girlfriend after my divorce was finalised and we have been happily married now for many years. Even to this day she occasionally says,

"I still have her number and I WILL call her again!"

****

Story 18.

The Unlucky War Veteran

Hi Peter, this story got to me and involves a guy called Mike from America, who was about seventy years old and a Vietnam War veteran. I was fed up with the bar scene in Bangkok.

I was sitting at a bar one morning about 11am on Sukhumvit Soi 21 having a Singha beer and noticed the old guy across the road sitting alone having a beer too. I went over and said hi to him and started chatting. He was a lovely man and spoke softly and told me he was married to a Thai lady just around the corner and she ran a laundry shop, I was excited to meet a new friend. He then went into the Vietnam War stories and was very interesting. I then noticed he had a false leg and as he was telling me the story, I could only imagine that he lost his leg in the war. I could not get a word in as he was on full flow with the war stories; eventually I got a word in and asked,

"So, you lost the leg in the war?"

He replied, "Hell no, last year I was out for a walk just on Sukhumvit Road and some motorbike crashed into me."

I thought, 'OMG, after surviving the war and getting on with life and this happened.'

I could only laugh so much, and he laughed too, of course there was no compensation ever. I continued to visit him most early mornings as he sat outside his wife's shop on his favourite chair having a coffee, I would sit and chat to him and he told me all about the girls, the fun and he now just likes to watch the world go by. I visited him quite a few more times and then I had to go back to China.

I returned to Soi 21 about three months later and called to see him. I was sad to see the empty chair outside the shop and asked about him, only to find out he had passed away.

After this and all the bad stuff that happened to me in the past, I prefer to go to Thailand and make friends with older expats and here their stories. So many stories out there. Tell this one only if you think its ok, I will do the other stories later. P.S, this was about four years ago. I also thought Soi 21 was a quieter Soi to chill out in.

****

Story 19.

Blindly Confused

This story was about me and a few of my friends on Walking Street, Pattaya. One of my friends has very poor eyesight without his glasses and my other friend is hilarious.

I arranged to meet them at a bar on Walking Street. I walked in about 10pm and noticed both of them but each at a different bar. My best friend was talking to a lady at one bar and seemed to be getting on well with her, but she told him she was busy that evening. As he got up and walked away from the bar, he turned to wave at this young lady then fell over a pool table which was behind him and the customers, together with the bar girls, all had a great time watching his performance.

He came to sit with me a bit flustered but no worse for wear. We noticed our other friend sitting at another bar (the one with bad eyesight), so we moved to a bar a couple of bars down from where he was sitting. After a short while he came to sit with us and said,

"Hi guys, how are you doing?"

Then he said to the waitress at this bar, "Where has my drink gone?"

She replied, "You haven't bought a drink."

He said, "I've been sat here for an hour and just went to the toilet. When I came back my beer has disappeared."

Then he told us that the woman a few seats down didn't waste much time chatting with another man, you can guess what he had done. He'd gone to the toilet, came back to the wrong bar, then complained he was being hard done by. I had to go back to the other bar and pay his bar bill. He's a bit older than us so no worries.

Just a short, funny story from a night out in Thailand, but obviously you had to be there to see the funny side of things.

****

Story 20.

Understanding Mama-San

I am an expat living in Israel with dual British and Israeli nationality. This time I really want to respond to last Saturday's story - one of eight - when you talked about the guy who was ripped off at a karaoke club. He had had too many drinks, had surrounded himself with a few girls in a closed room at the club, he consequently lost count of the number of drinks he had ordered and was presented with a bill for 40,000 Baht. Can't remember how he got out alive, but he did.

On my first trip to Thailand ten years ago, when I was sixty-five years old, I went with a friend who had already visited there many times. We stayed at a friend's condo in Chiang Mai, on the banks of the river Ping. My friend's experience and my own common sense had helped me then, and since on my frequent trips to the Land of Smiles. Subsequently I quickly sized up the situation regarding how I could enjoy myself and how I could avoid being scammed.

After the first three days of experiencing the joys of massage, I went looking for a karaoke club. I had no evil intentions in mind, just wanted to enjoy a few hours out in the company of the ladies while having a go at singing. Walking along the same bank of the river Ping about fifteen minutes from the condo, I came across a karaoke club with a line of about ten gorgeous ladies standing outside.

It was early evening, quite cold outside with a little bit of rain, and no other farangs wandering around on that main road. I approached a few of the ladies and engaged them in brief, casual conversation. However, I quickly discovered that only one of them, a good-looking girl in her early twenties, spoke good English. I thought she would be the only one to spend some time with. I wasn't going to sit in a closed room for two or three hours with someone who barely knew English. The one I chose was good looking, lively in conversation and had a pleasant demeanor. So, we went inside.

On the way in, the Mama-san showed us to our room. She was also in her early twenties and was a complete knockout. She was by far the most gorgeous girl I had seen since arriving in Chiang Mai. The Mama-san was unusually tall, and beautiful with long, black hair, and she wore a tight-fitting dress that enhanced her gorgeous figure. So, I thought I could talk with the nice girl I had met outside, I could perhaps dance with the Mama-san stunner and sing to both of them. Since there were no other clients either waiting outside, or evidently none inside, the Mama-san agreed to join me. This meant I would pay for the company of two girls and their ensuing ladies drinks.

Now one thing I haven't mentioned till now is this, despite the fact that this was my first time in Thailand, I knew when travelling abroad and particularly when walking around a strange city at night, I would never go out alone at night carrying more cash than I could afford to lose. Also, I never carried my credit cards with me at night.

I hadn't yet understood Chiang Mai. So, I assumed wrongly as it turned out, that I couldn't possibly wander into a bad district and be robbed. So, on that particular night I had less than two thousand baht in my pocket. Another thing is that I am not a drinker. I have diabetes and as we all know, alcohol has a high sugar content. So, another line of defense I have about not being robbed or scammed is that I am always sober. In fact, I get high on meeting beautiful ladies and enjoying their company while dancing and singing with them.

After being with these two gorgeous girls for about two hours and after they had drunk only a few ladies' drinks, I asked for the bill. It was brought into the room. I saw it was almost a thousand baht above what I had in my pockets. I had to make a quick decision. I turned to the Mama-san and told her that I couldn't pay that sum. She started to frown. I knew that I could either start an argument and say that the bill couldn't be that high, or I could take another line of approach. So, I said,

"Look I'm an old guy. I know that if I don't pay, you have the guys waiting outside to deal with difficult customers. We have enjoyed two great hours together. You are both wonderful people. I love Thailand and I think that I will come again with more money next time."

143

And anyway, there were no other customers. To underscore my situation, I pulled out my pockets and showed her all the cash that I had on me. She obviously realised there would be no point in getting the boys to rough me over.

So, she thought for a second and said,

"It's okay. You come back soon."

I paid and left after hugging them both and planting a kiss on their cheeks. I had not a single baht left in my pockets, but it was only a fifteen minutes' walk back to my friend's condo.

A week later, I spent my last three nights in Bangkok. Like all first-time male tourists, I headed for Patpong. I enjoyed the sights and sounds in the Go-Go bars. Finally, I found a crack-in-the-wall karaoke and live band bar on the upstairs veranda of what was probably Soi Cowboy or another one close by. The room was no more than three meters wide, about seven meters long, contained a male three-piece band, had a bar and six bar ladies. Yet again I found myself in an establishment as the only male customer. I ordered a non-alcoholic soda for myself and a lady drink for one of the girls.

After a second or third round of drinks, I asked the small band if they could play any Elvis songs. They said yes and I sang very bad renditions of a few Elvis numbers. Then I started dancing to heavy rock music with two of the girls.

As I already said I get high on dancing. In the middle of this high I saw a bell hanging above the bar. At the right point in the rhythm, I pulled the rope under the bell. A high ecstatic cheer went up from all the staff. I asked why they were all cheering. They explained that by ringing the bell I was ordering drinks all round. I responded by telling them that I as a non-drinker had not understood this. And yet again, it was understood that I was a newbie and a non-drinker.

They were all very nice about my lack of bar knowledge and said that they wouldn't charge me for drinks all round.

So, I bought just the band a round of drinks, had a few more dances and then left. All I am saying is that it doesn't pay to get drunk or let's say "blind drunk" in a strange land when you are out by yourself. And if you behave nicely and don't offend people, the Thais and even bar girls can show you that not every one of them is a scammer. They are just poor people trying to make a living in difficult circumstances. Most of the girls come from farming communities in the northeast of the country in the Issan province. Their parents, grandparents and children rely on these girls to send money home. They are not bad people. They are good people in difficult circumstances. The country's economy depends on tourism.

Whereas a large proportion of bar girls in the west working in clip joints and call-girls are either there to earn money to support a drug habit or even worse still have been trafficked by criminals, these local Thai girls are so devoted to their families that they are sometimes prepared to work in bars or as freelancers. I can't blame them. Having told you about my karaoke experience in the past, lastly, I want to give you a quick update about how Thailand is now after almost two years of the pandemic.

I haven't been able to visit there due to travel restrictions, but last week in mid-October 2021, my friend who had owned the condo in Chiang Mai, decided to fly to Phuket. Before leaving I told him that his trip would be a test case for me.

Since the epidemic hit worldwide and basically destroyed the tourist industry in Thailand, I wondered when it would recover and deal with the new reality. In 2019, I think Thailand had had about 20% - 30% of its income from tourism. But all of that had dried up. Every week I watch videos of the current situation. During this last month, efforts are being made by the Thai Tourist Authority to gradually reopen the country. Many YouTube channels optimistically report plans for renewal.

However, here is my update from my friend in Phuket. His WhatsApp response to my questions was this, on nineteenth of October,

"I'm so depressed (it will pass of course). This place compares to a favorite aunt that has developed Alzheimer's, MS, and Parkinson's since my last visit."

He included a few photos of empty streets in Phuket, and added,

"The first picture is the main entertainment street in Phuket at night when it's usually very busy (I'm not sampling the wares, my hotel is very near, honestly, scout's honour.) Look at all the closed places, McDonalds, Starbucks, Burger King etc."

Peter, I would have liked to end on a high note, but sadly this is the case. Will Thailand ever return to the tourist destination that we all love? What is your opinion, Peter?

****

Story 21.

Escape To a New Life

I was married for sixteen years and decided to get divorced because life was awful, and I thought that I would end up in a box! So, I had to decide on what I wanted to do once I left my wife. I decided that I wanted to travel. Soon afterwards I was doing singles holidays from the Canaries to the Caribbean.

At the time, I thought Thailand was full of sleaze, so no way that I was going to travel to Thailand. At the same time, I was involved in online dating, but I always found that the women on dating sites were looking for the next best thing and nothing worked out apart from the odd romance.

After a while I joined an Internet site called 'Companions to Travel' and after a few weeks, this lady called Sue contacted me and asked if I would join her on a holiday to Thailand via Dubai, where she wanted to spend twenty-four hours. So, without ever meeting Sue, we booked a flight to Thailand with Emirates, and we arranged to meet at Glasgow airport.

It was an amazing experience, we had only spoken on the phone and sent photos via email. So, we are now on our way to Thailand with the transfer in Dubai. On the flight from Dubai to Bangkok, Sue decided to have a sleep. When she woke up, she asked if there was any sign of the breakfast, I told Sue that she had missed it because she was asleep. Sue was not happy with me, so she went to the galley to ask if there was any breakfast left, only to be told that it would be served in 30 minutes. Sue was fuming with me! Anyways, three days in Bangkok and then a flight to Phuket for around seven days.

On the flight we sat next to an American guy who I will call Josh and honestly, he started to talk to the pair of us and tell us about our lives and he knew everything about us, our jobs and personal stuff that no one could ever know. It was shocking.

Anyway, we said our goodbyes at the airport and off we go to the hotel. What we found was amazing, we would meet Josh in the strangest of places in Patong in our hotel reception even though he wasn't staying there. There was a fortune teller stand where he was sitting chatting away to the fortune teller. Josh just had this gift he could tell your life story just by magic and I witnessed it when I had the odd night out with him, and he was talking to girls.

Now this story is absolutely true. We went out to an Italian restaurant in Patong that he had visited a couple of years before. Josh asked the lady if her husband was still around, she informed Josh that he had passed away recently. What was amazing is that Josh had told her on his last visit that her husband would not be around much longer and that he had an illness. Writing this story is bringing it all back to me. Anyway, myself and Sue used to chat with a few girls in the bars and spent time with them. The girls used to tell us the secrets of bar girls and the ways to drain a man's wallet, they also told us about the sponsors, some girls had four or five men sending them money and how it was difficult in keeping the men secret from each other. I thought, these girls are just conning men out of their money.

I was only on holiday to have a break and was not interested in going out with bar girls. I was enjoying time with my travel companion Sue and yes, we had separate rooms. The holiday soon came to an end, but I had another holiday with my travel companion in Egypt, which was OK, but we ended up falling out. She was a control freak once I got to know her, but I still keep in touch with Josh who lives in the USA.

After maybe six months later, I decided that I would have a good holiday in Asia starting in Kuala Lumpur, then Patong in Phuket and Bangkok before heading home. I had been introduced by email to a lady called "Diah" who lived in Kuala Lumpur by my American friend Josh who I met on the aircraft.

Diah arranged to pick me up at 7pm on the day I arrived to show me the sights. I was staying in the hotel over the road from the Times shopping mall. I arrived at the hotel at 4pm, the next thing I was asleep.

The phone rang, it was Diah. I told her that I had fallen asleep, and I said, I will be right down. Diah had her own 4X4 pickup truck. We said our hellos and she did a full tour of KL at night. She then had a surprise for me, she took me to this nightclub where a lady was having a birthday party and it was in the VIP area.

So here I was drinking and eating for free with total strangers. I got a lot of attention from the ladies, and I arranged to go out for dinner the following night with the birthday lady. The following day I did the sights, went up the tall communication's tower and after that I was back in town near to my hotel when the heavens opened, and it was like a monsoon.

While sheltering from the rain, I got talking to a Malaysian lady who started to tell me that her daughter was going to the UK and that she had won a place at Lancaster university, but she was scared about going to the UK. This lady told me that her husband was a chef and would I like to go to their house the following day for a meal to meet her daughter and to explain what to expect in the UK and Lancaster. Well, I said yes and arranged to be picked up outside of the Times shopping mall at 2pm the following afternoon.

That evening I was out with the birthday girl, and I told her that I was going out for dinner with a family whose daughter was going to the UK. The birthday girl told me not to go and that it was all a scam, and it is about gambling.

The following afternoon I was in the Times shopping mall, and I spotted the lady and two guys getting out of an old Proton car. I thought this looks dodgy, so I decided to hide in the shopping mail until they left. I must have been in there for over an hour and noticed that the car had gone. So, I made my way to the exit. I could not believe it, the lady was waiting for me and said,

"We have been looking for you!" She was not happy.

Rather than say "I wasn't going," I got into the back of this old Proton and was driven out of the city with this lady and two men. I asked if their daughter was in the house waiting, they told me that she had to go to the hospital and that she would be back later that day, but not to worry because her husband had cooked a nice meal for me.

I explained that I had to be back to the hotel at 7pm because I was going out for a meal with friends and that I didn't really want to eat too much. We arrived at the house and the husband was cooking chicken and rice, they offered me a drink, but I said no due to what they might put in the drink. I asked what time their daughter would arrive, but I did not get an answer. They told me that her uncle was upstairs and that he would like to have a chat with me, so he came downstairs and started to ask about what I did and if I ever go to the casinos… I told him that I never gambled and that I had never been to a casino. He then started to explain that he worked in a casino and with the help of me, we could win a lot of money together. I told him no, I am not interested, and I told the family that I didn't believe that their daughter was coming and that I wanted to be driven back to my hotel. They were not happy, but they agreed. So back in the car and they called into the petrol station, they filled up the car and told me that I had to pay for the fuel since they were driving me back, I reluctantly agreed. I got back to the hotel, but I could not believe what had happened and how easy it was to get sucked into a risky situation.

The lady knew I was from the UK, but she didn't know from where. For her to start talking about Lancaster university which is close to where I live was convincing and I guess she got lucky with her choice of city. I did not let this ruin my night.

I was out that night again with Diah and her friends and the following day I was off to Phuket. It was a great experience, and I did go back a few years later for the F1 race with a lady who would become my wife and it was nice to meet up with Diah again.

I managed to book into a nice hotel on the corner of Bangla Road and Beach Road, which was an ideal location. Now I am on my own and I can enjoy myself, I like my own company and I enjoy watching the world go by. It was just a matter of going out enjoying good Thai food, drinking, chatting with people, and enjoying the beach.

One day I decided to walk up a side Soi where there was a few bars and a lady shouted,

"Hello, welcome, come inside please, take a seat," but I walked on.

I don't know why but the girl who had shouted welcome to me stuck in my mind. Later that night, I decided to visit her bar. She was now working behind the bar, and it turned out that she was the cashier. The bar girls were hanging around me, but I wasn't interested in any of them and left. The following afternoon, I went back to the same bar. The cashier remembered me, and we had a good chat. She was setting the bar up, arranging the bottles and the bar stools. After that she started praying to the little Buddha shrine behind the bar, probably hoping that they would be busy that night. I had one drink and then left.

That evening I was back at the bar, and I got talking to an English guy whose wife used to work in the bar but was now living in the UK. They asked me if I was interested in any of the bar girls, I said the only girl that I was interested in was the cashier.

"No chance," they said. "She is too shy and won't go out with customers."

'Never mind,' I thought and carried on drinking.

The following night I was back at the bar and the English guy said that him and his wife were going to the beach the following day with the cashier and would I like to come along. I said yes and I guess the rest is history.

But I guess it is the start of the story, because the cashier, who I will call 'Bun,' who I found out was cooking breakfasts and other meals from 7am until 2pm and then she had to go and open the bar. The more I heard, the more I was shocked, she told me that sometimes, she would close up and fall asleep behind the bar. Honestly, the person who she was working for treated her like a slave with only a few hours of sleep a night and this was seven days a week. We didn't spend an awful lot of time with her, but I told her that she should consider moving on from that boss. The reason why she was there in the first place was to escape her ex-husband who was violent, and she had to get out of her village. He gambled their money away, drank and went with other women.

My holiday came to an end and within no time at all, I found myself back in the UK and back at work. I would phone 'Bun' every day and I arranged another holiday with her. She was still working at the same bar and at the restaurant during the day. Her boss was cunning, she owned a small guest house and would ask her customers to visit her bar. The bar girls would then hook up with her customers, she was onto a good thing.

Not only was her boss making money from the guest house, but her guests were spending in her bar and of course she got a cut from all the ladies drinks and kept the bar fines. However, on the plus side, the bar girls at this bar were making a very good monthly income.

I arranged to meet Josh in Patong, He was in Asia for six months during the winter months in the US. We were having a good time telling girls their fortunes and I now had a drinking partner. I could see that 'Bun' was very tired due to the amount of work she did. I asked her why she didn't go back home? She told me that she had bought a motorbike on a four-year payment plan, so she had to carry on working to pay off the loan. I asked her how much was outstanding on her motorbike? She told me about 25,000 Baht or £600, but she had 12,000 Baht or £300 in her back account. I offered to give her £300 if she put her £300 towards paying off her bike. 'Bun' and I headed off to the motorcycle dealership and we paid the bike off. We didn't really spend much time together due to her constant work, but I did give her a treat when I left, it wasn't much. I bought her a watch that she still has and gave her about £100 and then it was time to head back home and back to work. We kept in touch and 'Bun' told me that after she was paid, she was going to escape her boss and go back home to her village. She arranged to send her motorbike back to her village and she was getting the bus back home.

'Bun' was planning to work in the family shop in her village, plus her ex-husband now had a new, live-in girlfriend so he wasn't as much of a threat to her like before. I must say, in all this time, 'Bun' never once asked me for money. It was me who offered to give her money to pay off the bike and to leave Phuket.

After a few months, I was back in Thailand, and we arranged to have a holiday in Bangkok. It was at the time that the airport was shut down due to the yellow shirts demonstrating everywhere in the city, I got an extra week for free.

'Bun' was now working for her aunty in Bangkok, cooking for the family, 'Bun' was a self-trained cook. Her family had good money and her salary was OK with less hours. During this holiday 'Bun' mentioned that her family were not happy because I never sent or gave her any money apart from when I was leaving at the airport. I would tell her,

"Look, if we are getting on so well, maybe one day you won't need me to give you money because you might be living in the UK and that is much better than me sending you money."

The problem was that 'Bun' was losing face to her family, as I appeared to be a boyfriend to 'Bun' but a boyfriend who did not take care of her financially. I tried to arrange a Visa for 'Bun' to visit me in the UK, but the application was turned down.

'Bun' stopped working for her family and took a job in a food court in Pattaya, working twelve-hour days. She lived in a room with three other girls and tried her best to be frugal and save money. 'Bun' was a hard worker, and she was also supporting a son who was going to school, and she had high hopes of him going to university. I tried again to get 'Bun' a Visa to visit me in the UK and this time the application was successful, and 'Bun' had a Visa that allowed her to visit the UK for up to six months.

'Bun' arrived in the UK in October; it was a totally different climate to what she was used to, but she was seeing a brand-new world.

Everything we take for granted amazed her. She had never seen sheep in the fields or drinking water coming from the tap, my life turned upside down with 'Bun'. She would put toothpaste on my brush, I had fresh clothes to wear laid out on the end of the bed, cooked meals when I finished work along with a can of beer. I was waited on hand and foot. The morning came when 'Bun' was returning to Thailand, I had just finished night shift and was tired. I had to set off to the airport at 10am to take 'Bun' for her flight back home. I had contacted Emirates and changed her flight to the last day of her six months holiday Visa, and I also booked myself on the same flight. We decided to have a two-week holiday in Pattaya together.

A few holidays later, I managed to get 'Bun' another UK holiday Visa and to cut a long story short, at the end of her holiday, I asked 'Bun' to marry me while on a holiday in Manchester and she said yes. So, it was all planning, Marriage Visa's to check and we arrived in Bangkok.

I had to go the British Embassy to get the marriage papers and then off down the road to get them translated and then off to the Ministry of Foreign affairs and more papers translated. The following day we were married, I sent all the paperwork in for the Marriage Visa, and we went on a honeymoon to Koh Samui. Now, it was a waiting game for the Marriage Visa, and I had to go back home, it was strange leaving my wife alone in Bangkok airport.

Anyway, two weeks later 'Bun' was granted a Marriage Visa and I was off to Thailand to bring her back home to the UK. 'Bun' was happy to be called Mrs Smith and she was also happy to be back in our house that she now calls home.

During the last ten years since getting married, 'Bun' looked after my mother who passed away with Cancer. She looked after me after a stroke, I am OK now but retired at fifty-three and 'Bun' now works in a supermarket and is the breadwinner in our household. I have to say that I am one of the lucky ones, I never used to send money to Thailand and the money that I did give 'Bun' was small, but I always told her, if we hit it off, she would have a good life in the end. 'Bun' never sends money to Thailand; her family are doing OK with the family business. We are planning on 'Bun' becoming a British citizen which will be good for her if anything ever happens to me. I hope my story isn't too long and I hope that you can make sense of it all.

****

Story 22.

Dangerous Bar Girls

As described in my last story to you, the bars I am talking about are located in the South of Thailand, close to the Malaysian border and did not try to sell ladies drinks but rather "flowers" which were in fact a string of imitation flowers, each "flower" cost 100 Baht. So, if you liked a girl or wanted to have a chat or drink with her, you simply purchased one or more "plastic flowers" to give to the girl which she could exchange for cash later.

I was a regular, say two or three nights per week over a period of three years at these bars. In other words, many of the girls, bar owners, Mama-San's and bouncers knew me, and, in all instances, I think I was considered harmless and perhaps a little more generous than the average customer. There was this one particular girl, M, who I used to take out regularly for a couple months and then I got bored and went on to other girls. The first couple of times she saw me with other girls she would burst out crying like you have described many times in other stories. However, I never ignored her and always did buy her a few "flowers" every time I saw her and became friends rather than lovers. A few months later I saw her outside the bar and asked her would she like to join me and my friend for a meal, I guess it was her day off.

She said OK and after the meal she said she would take us to a bar where she did not work but had a couple of friends there. I agreed and off we went. I was also a regular customer of this bar, so all were welcoming, and the fun began. Once she saw a friend up on stage, she would ask me to buy them a "flower", which I agreed to do. This went on throughout the night and after a while, my friend and I decided to go back to our hotel, where we had already decided to meet some other girls who we had "booked" earlier that day. As we were leaving, we heard some commotion in the ladies toilet that was just outside the bar's entrance, which we ignored and walked off.

About an hour later my friend started knocking on my hotel door asking me to follow him out to look for M. I asked why? He told me that he had bumped into one of M's friends and she was hysterical saying that M had been beaten up by some girls at the bar we were in. I discovered later that the commotion we heard in the ladies toilet as we left that bar was M taken a beating.

We walked over to where M's friend stayed and discovered that she had been badly slashed with a razor blade and was in hospital. She was only discharged about a week later and used a lot of money for some plastic surgery in order for her to continue her bar girl career.

The reason for this assault was that she only asked me to buy "flowers" for her friends and did not encourage me to buy any for the other girls. I assume they were angry that they did not get to earn any "flowers" from me because of her influence and therefore decided to teach her a lesson.

I guess the moral of the story is to ensure no one loses face regardless of who they are, otherwise, their wrath can take on a very violent turn.

****

Story 23.

A Problem Gambler

Hello Peter, I've always enjoyed your "stories" segments but always considered myself lucky that I didn't have a story worthy of making it onto your channel. That recently changed and since I've enjoyed listening to the stories, I feel I should contribute as well. We can learn a lot from these stories, which is another reason I share it.

I moved to Khon Kaen in Isaan about a year ago. There's not a whole lot to do and the local scene feels a bit like, "been there, done that," rather quickly. For a bit of variety, I started to visit the neighboring cities of Udon Thani and Nong Khai. There's a train that runs from Khon Kaen to both cities and it's actually an enjoyable ride through the Isaan countryside.

On one of these trips to Nong Khai, I stumbled into one of the beer bars to shoot some pool. As you said in a recent video, the bar girls are fantastic pool players and I enjoy shooting pool with them. I grew up with a pool table in my home but got bored with the game over time as players you find in the bars back home are generally average and with little challenge the game can get boring. Like I'm sure many of the viewers and readers here, I became humbled quite quickly after initially thinking I could walk into these bars in Thailand and beat the best girl in each bar. I'm not ashamed to admit that I've been schooled by these girls on many occasions at the pool table. I enjoy playing the girls for drinks. It ensures you get their best game and the girls have been the ones buying me drinks on quite a few occasions. Win or lose though, I usually end up buying them a few drinks regardless. At the end of the day, I'm there for fun and they are there to make money, but they seem to be having fun as well.

Many of the girls that leave the scene often return, and sometimes it's not because of money. I've known quite a few that were being taken care of by their farang boyfriends but couldn't handle staying at home and missed the bar scene, often returning to it despite not needing the money.

I walked into a beer bar in Nong Khai and took a seat at the bar. I swiveled around to watch the girls all playing pool together, and one of them really caught my eye. She seemed to be late twenties with a stunning body. She was wearing one of those Chinese gowns that had nothing but lace going up the left side, so you could see a bit of her body from head to toe and she was in fantastic shape. We kept locking eyes and smiling. I've been around the block, so chalked this up to what it usually is, flirting to get the drinks going. I had a few drinks and decided to check out some of the other bars but kept thinking about that fantastic body and smile. I soon found myself back in the bar just in time for a tournament of killer. Killer Pool is a popular game here in Isaan that usually has the whole bar playing with a nice mix of Thai and farangs, including many local Thai men who enjoy drinking and shooting pool in these bars also. Everyone puts in 100 Baht and gets three marks. You lose a mark when you miss a shot. Last one standing wins the pot.

This time the last one standing was the Mama-San. All those years in the bars had really developed her into a sharp player. After the game I started playing with the girl I was there for and bought her a few drinks. We really clicked well together and there was no doubt, she was the one I wanted to see for more drinks back at the hotel. I gave the usual, "let's get out of here," to get the ball rolling, but she seemed caught off guard and asked me to stay until her shift was over at midnight.

The bar scene here during the pandemic feels like a throwback to the times of prohibition. We all must drink from coffee cups or with a zero-alcohol bottle next to our cups and the aluminium doors roll down at 10 o'clock, but we continue behind closed doors. With the doors down, the girls will sometimes start to panic and get everyone to stay still and quiet while the lights go off. They've picked up the scent of the police rolling down the street. It's a bizarre experience that makes me think, this is what it must have felt like back in the 1920's. It's doubly bizarre knowing that everyone knows what's going on, including the badges rolling by outside, but they are all playing their part in the charade.

Like many things here in Thailand, the rules are selectively enforced and a lot of what goes on is just for show. I'm getting off track quite a bit, but I think these points might give viewers and readers some insight into things that normally don't get discussed or that are unique to these times.

The aluminium doors rolled down and Nee and I continued to play pool. I thought maybe she was trying to save me the bar fine by waiting a bit longer, which is something the girls will sometimes do. So, midnight rolls around and I'm like, 'great, now let's go,' but she wants to stay longer and is behaving in a very coy way. There is no talk of money and the whole thing just feels out of sorts from how this usually goes down.

Viewers and readers should know that not all girls leave with customers, and they shouldn't take offense if a girl won't leave with them, as some just don't do it and are content with the money they get from drinks. I was thinking maybe she was one of these girls, but they will almost always tell you this the moment you mention wanting to leave with them.

She seemed very conflicted about staying or going and I finally said,

"I'm leaving. If you want to stay, then stay, if you want to go, then let's go…"

Then gave her the often-used expression here in Thailand,

"Up to you."

"Wait five minutes," she said. "I want to change and get my things."

I'm thinking, 'well, what was so hard about that.'

She changes, still looking stunning, and we leave. She needs to head back to her nearby apartment for some more things. Again, I'm finding this odd as the girls are usually well prepared. After that, she wants to get some food. I'm thinking, is she trying to milk me for all I'm worth? The whole thing feels like she is delaying things and she is acting like a nervous girl on prom night.

We finally make it back and she wants to eat, drink, and talk. No, I mean actually drink. Again, this feels like more delay tactics, and it feels like she's never done this before. It's all odd to me and I'm getting a bit frustrated. She showers and despite her nerves we end up having a great 'time.'

I leave a small gift on the nightstand and expect she will be gone soon. But she's got all her stuff to stay overnight and seems to expect she will be sleeping here and despite my never mentioning it, I wanted an overnight guest. Again, I find this odd and also find it odd that she didn't bring any protection but expected me to wear some. Again, these girls are usually prepared for everything, but she didn't seem prepared for anything. I went to sleep.

At about 2am, I wake up and see she is playing roulette on her phone. I think, 'she can't sleep and is playing a phone game,' no big deal. I wake up another couple hours later and she is still playing and seems to be getting upset. I take a closer look and see that this is an online casino. She grabs the gift I left and asks me to walk with her downstairs. I have no idea what's going on but out of curiosity I agree. She heads out the lobby and a motorbike with two people pulls up. She hands them the money, they watch each other, and then the motorbike speeds off. Ahhhhh, it's dawned on me. They're collectors for the casino. I worked in the casino business for twelve years and roulette has one of the biggest advantages for the house. I've witnessed Roulette destroy people financially a number of times over the years.

We head back up and I fall back to sleep. I wake up at about 7am, and she is still playing roulette. Whoa, this should have been a huge red flag that should have prevented me from what was to come, but we're all human and I still make mistakes.

I try to explain to her about my experience working in casinos and how roulette is a losing proposition in the long run. I feel bad for her because after so many years in the casino, an addict is pretty easy to spot, and I know where it leads.

I have a train to catch, so a few hours later we say our goodbyes and part ways. I don't think much of it over the next coming days, it was after all, a nice little adventure.

Life starts to get stale again back in Khon Kaen and I decide to once again catch the train. It feels like a rare adventure to take during these times, and you get to let loose a bit more in a place where you don't live, so I feel a bit like an excited kid when I take these trips. I think about Nee and decide to head over to her bar and say hi. I walk in and she is having drinks with some customers over at a table. Her eyes light up when I enter, and I feel that the chemistry we had was not just something my imagination had crafted. I grab a seat at the bar and decide to have a few beers, listen to the music, and let her do her thing. I'm an adult and have no problem moving on if she's busy. It's part of the game. Shortly after my arrival, she breaks from the group and saddles up next to me.

A few drinks in, I mention I want to go bar hopping, tell her it was great seeing her again, and then gather myself to leave. She grabs my arm and says,

"I'm going with you."

Grabs her stuff and we are out the door. I'm thinking, what about needing to stay until midnight like before? But I don't mention it and no transactional conversation ever took place. Again, it's odd. We hop a few bars and have a great time together. We really have some great chemistry and that translates into great chemistry back at the hotel. We drink late into the night back at my hotel. I sleep soundly and awake at about 8am… to the sight of Nee playing roulette on her phone and smacking her forehead in frustration. More lectures from me that I know will fall on deaf ears, but I can't help but think my time in the casino business might pull a little more weight and have a chance to help her. I can explain to her things about the game she doesn't understand. While some gamblers know the odds and continue, I know from my time in the business that many don't and that she almost surely doesn't.

It's a sad fact that many of the girls in the bars are under educated. She finally falls asleep. I leave a gift on the nightstand and prepare to catch the train out of town. I kill a few hours and then wake her to give her a kiss goodbye. She's confused about my gift on the nightstand. She says,

"You paid for all the food and drinks last night, why are you giving me this?"

I'm thinking, 'is this a put on?' I say,

"It's a gift for you."

She tries to give it back. I'm thinking, 'No need for a show here, just take it.'

But she keeps persisting. Eventually I convince her that it will stay on the nightstand whether she takes it or not, kiss her goodbye, and head out of town.

We text back and forth quite often after that. She says she wants me to have the money back that I had gifted her and asks for my bank account number so she can transfer it to me.

Viewers and readers should know that exchanging account numbers for this purpose is not uncommon in Thailand. But, whoa, I'm very skeptical. Even though we are now beyond being acquaintances and I trust her, there is no way I am giving my bank account number to a gambler. I know how crafty an addict can be and I'm not taking any chances. I'd rather she has the money anyway.

We chat every day and I eventually learn that she had only been working in the bar for a month and had never left with anyone before or since. Now I know what some of the vets are thinking,

'Ahh, come on mate, what a mug!"

But I am no rookie and am just as skeptical about this stuff as the crusty old vets. All the things I found odd before finally started to add up and yeah, I believe her. Not because of what she said, but because of all the circumstantial evidence based on her actions and behaviours. I'll say I am in good shape, above average looking, and carry a conversation with women better than most guys at the bar, in case anyone is trying to find a reason for why she broke her ways for me. She was also becoming way more attached than other girls I've chatted with before.

She was constantly wanting to video chat. It was becoming a bit smothering, but because we'd had so much fun together, I endured more of it than I normally would. I've always said I would never date a bar girl. The cautionary tales we hear on your channel being one of many reasons.

When she mentions wanting to come to live with me, I'm like whoa, pump the brakes.

"First off, I am not going to support you or give you a 'salary' like some farangs do. You can come here for a week, and we can see how it goes. I'll pay for all the food and drinks, but that's it."

My gut was telling me it was a bad idea, but below the gut I was thinking, 'this could be fun for a week.' She is not Thai. She is from one of the border countries and she was asking if you need ID to get a train ticket or if they check IDs on the train. There are a lot of people living in Thailand from the border countries and not all of them are "up to date" on their Visas, and it's becoming apparent she can't just hop on the train.

My gut was telling me, "This is your out!"

Below, the gut was telling me, 'Just rent a car, drive up there and bring her here.'

I tell her if I do this, she has to promise to stop playing Roulette. She agrees and I'll note that I never saw her play it again. I rent the car, make the drive, and we have a wonderful drive back, it felt like we were newlyweds.

The beginning of a relationship is always the time I enjoy most. We get back and while I am out getting food for us, I get a text asking me to pick up some sanitary napkins. That time of the month has just begun.

'Oh, for Pete's sake! I can't believe my luck!'

Obviously, this is not something you can't fake so I knew it wasn't an excuse to avoid aerobic exercise and while she had been shy the first night, the second night she had been more eager than me. At least she was great company and loved giving me fantastic strong massages for literally hours on end.

She really treated me great. I was even thinking, 'I know what I've said in the past, but this might go somewhere.'

Besides, I think I can make an exception considering the circumstances which had come to light about her being a drinks only girl.

I've had a few weeks to distance myself from the situation and yes, I firmly believe she was being honest about that the more I have thought about it. Despite it being that time, I decided to make the best of the situation and still have a great week together. She made sure I was happy in other ways.

The second night we decided to go out for a few drinks and check out the local scene. We had a good time for a few hours then returned home. This is where our story takes a turn for the worst!

Upon arrival her personality does a complete turn and she starts screaming at me in Thai. I can't understand why she is mad, but she is furious about something. Through translation apps I learn she is now listing off a dozen things I have done wrong. These mainly stem from jealousy issues. She is mad about photos of my ex being on my phone. She is mad about me glancing at another woman in the bar. She is mad... well, it turns out, she is just mad.

She proceeds to hang out on the balcony and yell all night at me in Thai. I try pleading with her to stop, I don't understand what she is saying, and I have no idea why she is this angry. I have a view of the courtyard which echoes horribly, and the entire community can surely hear her. The only bright side I can see is that because she is yelling in Thai, the neighbors might think it is a local couple having a row. In one of these outbursts, she suddenly breaks for the kitchen, grabs a knife and starts charging me… Time slows down…I can't believe this is happening.

My mind is suddenly split as I process what is happening. Part of me in fight or flight mode, the other part is thinking,

'Oh, this is a female Thai move I've read about enough times to know it's just a tactic they like to use to get your attention.'

Tactic or not, I'm not taking any chances. She is literally half my size, and it takes little effort to wrestle her to the bed and take the knife away. I proceed to gather up all the sharp objects in the house and place them out of reach from her.

Hours of her yelling continue and as the sun is rising, she is finally starting to tire. She assures me I can go to sleep because she really loves me and wouldn't hurt me. Oh well that certainly puts my mind at ease, I'll sleep like a log. After I hear her start to snore, I eventually fall asleep as well.

I wake up thinking… 'How the hell am I going to get rid of her? I can't just put her on a train or bus. She can't use her ID. Shit, I'm gonna have to drive her back and I want it done quickly.'

No way do I want her staying any longer than necessary. But I need to work so it needs to wait a day. I mention that I will take her back, but she is insistent on staying the week and apologies profusely. She's literally at my feet begging forgiveness. I need to buy at least another day, so I tell her she is forgiven and hope that it's just an issue related to it being that time of the month and that it won't happen again. I tell her that it can't happen again or I'm calling the cops. This carries extra weight, or I think it will, because she can't be showing her ID. I finish work and hope for the best.

She is being especially sweet and trying to salvage things as best she can. I soon start to feel comfortable again and we head out for dinner. Things surely aren't going back to the newlyweds' stage again, but I do manage to let her back into the fold, slightly. If for no other reason, than to make the drive back less miserable than I already anticipate it will be. We get home that night, and she is about to slip into bed wearing the same clothes she was wearing when we were out and about. I'm a bit of a neat freak and ask her to change her clothes and shower before bed, explaining that it's a quirk of mine and that during these times we should be more sanitary anyway. Whoa, she takes this the wrong way.

She thinks I have insinuated that she is unclean, takes horrible offense, and starts screaming at me in Thai again. I explain,

"Look, you saw me do the same thing, it's a rule I hold myself to as well."

She won't listen to reason, and I see that last night wasn't just a fluke. For whatever reason, she just wants to fight, and the reasons don't matter. I have absolutely no tolerance for this.

I have to hatch a plan and end this as soon as possible. The night proceeds with her threatening to jump off the balcony several times. I stop her the first few times.

I'm thinking, 'Yep, another tactic I've read about many times. She's probably not serious, but I'm not taking any chances.'

Eventually I'm just too exhausted and lay in bed looking at the ceiling, wondering if I'm going to hear the screaming of a jumper but knowing damn well I won't.

Not getting the attention she wants, she now says,

"I'm leaving," and proceeds to start packing, hoping I will try and stop her.

I'm frozen in bed, praying to all the Gods out there, please, let this be the one thing she is being sincere about. I'm mentally prepared to rush to the door and lock it the minute I hear it close. But of course, it never opens. Normally I would call the police in this situation, and I threaten to. But I don't do it, because even though she is making my life hell, I don't want her getting into the trouble that would await her if I did that.

As the sun rises, she finally exhausts herself. Yes, she stayed up all night yelling because I asked her to wear pyjamas in bed and not our street clothes. I need to think fast. This can't go on. I call in sick and grab the nearest rental car I can find. I had given her a second chance. I know she will refuse to leave again. I need to come up with a plan. I say to myself,

"Come on Bob think! You can come up with an idea."

When she wakes, I explain to her that this isn't going to work out and that I will be taking her back today. As I predicted, she immediately starts refusing and begging for forgiveness.

I launch my plan and I explain, "Look, you lost the second chance. I told you that if you behaved like that again I was taking you home."

I explained to her that I've always kept my word to her and that this was not going to be an exception. I am keeping my word again and she will be leaving, but calm down, I have an idea.

"You blew the second chance, but I'm giving you a last chance. I'll take you home and I will see you on weekends. But it's your last chance, if we fight again, it will be over."

She seems to understand that it's this deal or nothing and finally relents. As I am packing, she inquiries about me leaving some things at her place since I will be coming to stay on the weekends. I've no choice but to sell this so I say,

"Of course!"

And begin to pack some things she knows I can't live without. I'm sure I can casually transfer some of them into my daypack once we arrive. I somehow survive the drive back, and believe me, I am sick of bouncing back between these two cities at this point.

I unpack my stuff and put on my best Academy Award performance that evening and leave the next day, successfully transferring the things I need without notice. I get home and breathe a sigh of relief, it's over.

The next day I go to grab one of those items I must have, and gulp, it's not there. There were two items that I can't part with I had accidentally left behind. How could I have been so careless. I can't believe this, I'm actually gonna have to go back as I had said I would in my plan.

I take the train back that weekend and she is bubbling with joy, saying she was worried I had only said those things to get rid of her and would abandon my things. Again, I aim for the Oscar with my acting, but now I need to do it not just verbally, but physically. It's going to be another night of fighting if I don't sell it.

Fortunately, despite me not being mentally attracted to her anymore, I was still very much physically attracted to her and had no problems pulling off this final act, or acts. I had casually retrieved the items I needed and was waiting for my chance to escape the next morning.

After waking she began asking me about my ex. After this went on for a bit, she was getting pushy about it, I used it as the reason for her losing her last chance. I grabbed my bag, threw on my shoes, and bolted for the door. Of course, she tried to stop me, but being half my size, I easily brushed her aside and began walking hurriedly down the street. About a hundred meters later I hear her screaming,

"Darling! Darling,"

I look back to see her running after me. She's like the Terminator, she just won't give in.

I began running knowing she can't catch me. She quickly gives up and as luck would have it, the next train is leaving soon. I run all the way to the train station and quickly buy a ticket. In the station I find a spot where a passerby can't see in, for fear she will try and find me. She is texting me non-stop and I warn her that I will need to block her. She dares me to, so I do. What a relief.

Over the next few weeks, she will update her Line profile and timeline with messages and photos clearly aimed at getting me to unblock her. You can still see those when you've blocked someone.

The train pulls away and I can finally relax. It's over. To kill time, I put on my headphones and pull up YouTube.

No lying, one of your "Viewer Stories" episodes has just come out and I have a listen. Enjoying it as usual and about halfway through it dawns on me,

"Crap, I think I have a submission!"

Story 24.

Tattoo for Two

I thought I might tell a funny Bangkok story that happened to me, this was all a few years ago. Many of the details are fuzzy except for the punchline in the end.

I am a Singaporean in my forties now who went to Thailand several times a year, mostly for work. When I had time, I would spend most evenings in the nightlife areas. Sometimes I would take a Go-Go or bar girl out, but always tried to keep in mind about the nature of the ensuing relationship in case some feelings crept up unawares. I've been to Nana Plaza on Sukhumvit Soi 4 quite a lot. I sometimes went to the most popular Go-Go bar there at the time, but not as often as I would have liked. The ladies there are mostly good-looking, but it was far too crowded & the waitresses can be too pushy.

However, on one visit there was a Go-Go dancer who was so attractive I could not get her to sit at my table and drink with me. She had these features resembling a particular South Korean popstar/actress. This was in contrast (which I liked a lot) to her very elaborate multicoloured tattoos on her body, tattoos of birds, including a gorgeous peacock or phoenix going down to her calves.

Let me call her Ms Tattoo. I asked if she'd like to come to my hotel room & she said yes. I did not feel like taking a taxi there as my hotel was located in the middle between Nana & Soi Cowboy. We walked, but halfway to our destination it began to rain a little, so we hurried along. This ended being a minor mistake as Ms Tattoo had high heels on. When we arrived at my hotel building, I noticed her cheerful mood had reduced by about 20%. To sort of 'reset' the situation, I thought we might take a quick drink down at the hotel's basement bar. The bar, which is world-famous, was filled to the brim with ladies. Ms Tattoo was very curious about the establishment. I'm sure a few of your viewers and readers know about this basement bar. After our drink, we left to go up to my room. On the elevator ride there she asked me a lot of questions. She had never heard of that basement bar. From her facial reactions to my answers, it appeared she was making a mental note to return to the bar with a few of her Go-Go lady friends later to try their luck.

She was even more beautiful in my room. Come to think of it, she was probably the most gorgeous women I had ever been with up to that point. I had a splendid time, but had problems completing the deed, due to having drunk a little too much that night. My delay seemed to upset her a bit. I had to convince her that 'It was me not her'. But I hoped to see her again on my next trip.

Back home in Singapore I would sometimes catch myself daydreaming about her. I looked for her again during the proceeding trip, but she was gone. I did not memorize her badge number, so I had no choice but to put it down as one of those single happy memories to cherish. I tried not to let my missing her & the regret overwhelm me. Her Go-Go bar closed due to some issue. It then reopened a few months later, then changed locations, then confusingly had two locations in the new and in the previous place.

One day a few years later I was at the new Go-Go location and suddenly saw Ms Tattoo there in the corner. She was busy entertaining some other customers & did not notice me. From what I could see she had not changed a lot. She still had the same tight body & the tattoos. Finally, after about half an hour of trying to get her attention, I asked one of the waitresses to ask Ms Tattoo directly whether she would like to go with me. The waitress sent the message. I saw Ms Tattoo look back. Locking eyes with me, she smiled sweetly. Yes, she remembered me. My heart sparked with joy. Instead of going to my place, which was far away, we went to a nearby hotel about five minutes from Nana. In the hotel room, before I went to shower, I gladly remarked how pleased I was to see her as I thought we would never meet again. I said that I thought she stopped working at the Go-Go or went to work somewhere else when it closed.

When I returned from showering, I noticed she still had her clothes on & still held her handbag & wore her shoes. Was she preparing to leave? For a second, I thought I had been scammed in some way. She said she had something important to tell me. She said this was the first time we'd ever been together. I was at first surprised & was a bit hurt by this. So, she really had forgotten me, which I can understand could be normal as Go-Go girls meet many people. Then she took out her smartphone and showed pictures of another girl, who looked a lot like her. It turned out that I went out with her elder sister many years ago. They really did look a lot alike. I even had to ask her twice whether they were actually twins, not just sisters. They even had the same type of multicoloured bird tattoo, only that this younger Ms Tattoo's was not as elaborate or big. I began laughing hard & she did too. Somehow this established a closer rapport between us. She asked whether I still wanted to be with her. I said yes. She beamed with delight. Our time in that hotel room was more relaxed. The younger Ms Tattoo had a more playful demeanor than her sister. Her face was constantly smiling widely and warmly. Every few minutes I had to stop & laugh again at my mistake & at this strange turn of events in which we found ourselves. She told me that her sister was away for two to three years but might return. Even today I still did not know what that meant. Maybe the older sister was at school. Or maybe she was overseas for a temporary period. Or maybe she was married to someone & was planning to end it in two to three years. But I did not ask further. I never did see either of them again. I guess the relationship would have quickly turned awkward if I ever encountered the two sisters together. But what a strange coincidence.

****

Story 25.

"I Want to Go Home"

This is a story of one of the many nights I've spent in Pattaya over the last fifteen years. It begins like any other night in Pattaya, bar hopping and out on the prowl in the hope of finding some female company. It ends, however, with no sordid accounts, but instead one of the many experiences that have shaped my understanding of Thailand and its people.

On this night, I found myself in one of the more 'friendlier' establishments on Walking Street. As soon as I sat down, one of the lovelies on stage caught my eye. They were all lovely to be fair, but I had a particular type, which this girl happened to fulfill. A pretty girl by any account. She strutted her stuff as they do in this place. I did notice, however, that compared to all the screaming and tomfoolery going on all around me, she did seem a little glum. I was already taken by her at this point, so I called her over to my table anyway. I did my best to win her over while she sipped on her lady drink, but again, something seemed off. Finally, she leaned over to my ear and confessed that she's not feeling well and won't be able to join me tonight. Though disappointed, I also knew that other options were just down the road. I smiled and simply spent the rest of my time in the bar genuinely having a friendly chat with this girl. I naively asked why she didn't just call in sick if she was unwell? She explained that being a weekend, no leave was allowed. The only way out was if she was bar fined by a customer.

Of course, I knew what was coming. She asked if I could bar fine her so she could go home. I was about ready to make my excuses and move on, when she further explained that she could afford to pay for half and swore she would pay me back the rest somehow. I stared into her eyes, put my hand on her forehead, and realised she did indeed have a fever. I knew I was not getting my money back. I called the Mama-San over to make the arrangements. The girl then discreetly stuffed a ball of cash into my hands and went off to get her things. It was about 400 Baht in crumpled notes; her takings for the night I supposed. I paid the full bar fine together with our drinks and was soon walking her out to Second Road. Along the way, she kept thanking me profusely, while tightly holding my hand.

We reached Second Road and I asked her, "What will you do now?"

"I call my brother. He come take me home."

"Ok then..."

"Your money, I pay you back. How long you stay Thailand?" She interrupted.

"No, it's ok. I have to go," I responded.

"No wait... I take care of you... I come your hotel now, ok?"

"No really, it's ok. Go home and get well," I said.

After an awkward pause, this "lovely girl" started tearing up, got down on her knees, and bowed to me in the Thai fashion, for all of Second Road to see. It took all my strength to hold in my own tears, as I quickly picked her up and hugged her. We waited till her brother arrived and said our goodbyes. I never saw her again and wondered at first if I'd been had. But I soon concluded for myself that it didn't matter. I did what I could, given the situation, with a few hundred Baht less, but with another story

to tell, of the land and people we've come
to love.

****

Story 26.

Just Good Friends

This story is about my recent trip to Phuket. I met a lady at one of the clubs on Bangla Road. She used to work in the bar scene until she gave that up just over a year ago. We instantly clicked and then spent the rest of my trip together.

She used to come to my hotel in the morning to take me to different beaches every day where we spent the entire day. She then used to drop me back to my hotel in the evening and we used to meet again after a couple of hours for dinner or drinks. She told me that she didn't know what she wanted to do in the future with regards to work. She also told me that presently she was not looking for romance. I think the reason she spent so much time with me is because I never asked her about money or charges for her company and we just got on really well and were kind of like good friends. We were inseparable; and every bar we visited regularly, people asked me if she was my wife or girlfriend. We interacted in such a way (without being touchy feely), that people thought we were a couple. I paid for all the drinks, food and entertainment when we were together, this is of course normal in Thailand or thinking about it, most of the world if you are dating.

Since I met this lady I never bar fined anyone while in Phuket and she never entered my room at my hotel, we were never intimate with each other.

I started to have genuine feelings towards her, and I told her so. She told me that she loved the time we had spent together, and she always felt safe when with me, but she also went on to tell me that she wanted nothing more than friendship from our relationship.

I returned to Australia and for a while we were in constant communication however, she suddenly stopped replying to my texts and to be honest, I feel extremely hurt because I feel like whatever I thought we had, was just business for her. It looks like she just wanted to go out every day and have a good time at my expense and I now wonder if our conversations were really manful for her as they were for me. Of course, we exchanged many personal details about each other as trust started to grow over time.

I know this isn't really much of a story and I am not presuming that you are a relationship expert, but I have been watching your videos for a while now and you do seem very experienced about Thailand. Can I ask you, based on what I have explained above what do you think her motivation was? Was it all a lie to keep me engaged or did she really enjoy my company?

I am of Indian origin but have been living in Sydney Australia since 1992. I am thinking of moving to Phuket within the next two or three years and hoping to make a business or investments. I intend to continue visiting Phuket two or three times a year for now and until I move out their full time.

****

Story 27.

Joys of Life

I would like to tell you a story about a friend I introduced to Thailand. This story spans over eight years and it's all true.

I first visited Thailand with my girlfriend in the early 1990s, we had been living in Australia so stopovers on trips back home were always an option, I didn't get to sample all Thailand had to offer but I enjoyed the country, food and beaches immensely.

After we'd split up, I had spent about a year working in Bali before returning to the UK and got to sample a little of what Southeast Asia has to offer.

Back living in the U.K. I had an uncle living in Bangkok and a friend I'd known in Australia before he moved to Pattaya and opened a bar. We were still in touch, and he told me to come over for a holiday.

I had not visited Pattaya on my previous trips so had no idea what to expect. It was a few years before I got the chance but when the opportunity presented itself, I took a two-week holiday in Bangkok and Pattaya and I had the time of my life and became a regular visitor to Thailand.

I had a friend in the UK I'd known for over twenty-five years; we had travelled all over the world when we were younger living out of each other's pockets and on telling him of the great times I was having in Pattaya he asked if I'd take him next time I went. I was visiting Pattaya up to five times a year by then so on my next trip we went together.

My friend called Fred had a young son and was separated from his partner, he's a big guy with a huge beer belly and a smile like stone. He's never really been that successful with the ladies, so I was pleased to be taking him with me to Thailand.

I explained in great detail how it all worked, bar fines, long and short times, what the girls will say, how to avoid being scammed, what the scams were, etc. I told him I only ever met-up with a girl for one day, I didn't try to develop long term relationships. I advised him to just do the same and have a good time on his first visit.

We landed in Bangkok at about 9pm and once through customs and into a taxi we arrived in Pattaya by about 11.30pm. I had booked a hotel on Soi 8 in the middle of the action as a way of introducing Fred to Pattaya and thought we would stay there for a few days then move on. As our taxi pulled into Soi 8, I watched his jaw drop, he couldn't believe his eyes. Hundreds of beautiful women screaming and dancing. His face was a picture. I thought this is going to be a fun few weeks.

We checked in, took a shower and were out of the hotel before midnight. We walked across to Soi 7 then walked down towards the Beach with Fred completely mesmerised. We stopped at a bar at the end of the Soi for our first beer and sat at the bar. One of the girls started talking to Fred and was coming out with the usual lines that bar girls come out with.

"Where you from? How long you stay Pattaya? How many time you come to Thailand? You want play game? …"

All the usual chat-up. We drank our beers and I said,

"Let's go to my friends' bar," as I wanted to introduce Fred to my friends.

"No," Fred said, because he really liked the girl he has been talking to and would

202

I ask her if she would go back to his hotel with him for drinks?

"Relax. We have only just arrived; we can come back later if you like."

He said, "No. I really like her; would you talk to her for me."

'Whatever,' I thought. 'The guy was desperate.'

So, I spoke to the girl he was drinking with, who turned out to be called Joy. Within a few minutes they were heading back to the hotel. We had only been in Pattaya for an hour or so, is this a record?

Anyway, I went and did my own thing, visiting friends and bar hopping. When I got back to the hotel, outside of Fred's room were a stack of room service trays and a do not disturb sign on the door.

The next day I got up around 1pm and headed down to the pool. I could see our rooms from the poolside chair I was lounging in. Fred's curtains were drawn and there was no sign of him. I chatted with a few of the guys by the pool, had some food and a few beers. Fred eventually emerged at around 5.30pm, I have never seen a happier man in my life. He came bounding over telling us what a great time he had and how the night had been amazing. I was delighted for him and the other guys round the pool thought it was hilarious to see someone so happy after his first night in Pattaya.

Then Fred said there was a problem! 10,000 Baht had disappeared from his room! I told him to speak with the hotel manager.

Fred said, "No, it probably wasn't Joy."

I asked who else could it be? He said he didn't know, then the other guys who were there all told Fred to go and try to get your cash back.

Fred just said, it wasn't her and that was it.

OK fine, it's his money, his choice. Then Fred said,

"I have to go now."

"Where to?" I asked.

He said he had arranged to go back to Joy's bar.

Everyone at the pool said, "But she's just robbed you."

But off he went anyway.

The next day was exactly the same, Fred came down at 5.30pm when Joy had to go back to the bar. He was as happy as ever. He told me how wonderful everything was and what an incredible time he'd had but there was just one problem, another 10,000 Baht was missing from his room! Once again, myself and the guys around the pool said,

"Go and get it back!

Fred again refused to blame Joy and became angry.

He started saying things like, "She's not like the other girls here. She's different and I love her."

With that he left to go back to her bar once again. To be honest I couldn't believe what I was hearing, here was someone I had known for years who I thought I knew well. The other guys around the pool couldn't believe it ether.

Fred had been in Pattaya for less than forty hours, had 20,000 Baht stolen from him and was professing love for a bar girl he had just met. Has he totally lost his head?

The rest of the holiday didn't go well, the routine was the same every day. He spent two weeks either in Joy's bar or in the room with her. I foolishly lent him 40,000 Baht which he swore on his son's life he'd pay me back as soon as he got home. Once back in the UK, I called him and asked for my money back.

Fred made every excuse under the sun as to why he could not pay me back straight away. Then one day Fred called me and told me he was very happy because he had bought a ticket to go back to Pattaya.

"Where is my money? I asked him.

He told me, "You don't need it right now, but I need every penny I can get my hands on."

Needless to say, what had once been a close friendship ended right there! Fred has ripped me off for a Pattaya bar girl, I was totally disgusted with him.

I didn't see Fred for about three years after that until one day back in Pattaya I was walking along the Beach Road and who comes walking towards me; it was Fred and Joy! Time is a great healer and out of curiosity more than anything we all arranged to meet up for a beer later that evening.

Joy was still working in the bar, so Fred and I met up in another bar close by. He told me how they had become extremely close and were getting married.

I said, "But she's still working in the bar."

He said, "She doesn't go with customers, she only accepts drinks and tips..."

I thought, 'of course she does.'

Anyway, we made our way back to her bar and ordered a couple of beers.

At the end of the night, we asked for our separate bills. My bill was 60 Baht for one beer, but Fred's bill was 2,150 Baht.

Joy had ordered lady drinks for her and all her friends and put it on Fred's bill.

Fred said, "Not again, what are you doing to me?"

And all this after Fred had been telling me how close they were, the guy was a deluded idiot.

I said my goodbyes and left the bar. I thought, 'you deserve all you've got.'

A few days later after Fred had gone home, I was walking down Soi 7 when Joy had seen me and came running out of her bar. She said to me,

"I go with you."

I didn't take her up on her offer however thinking about it, the 40,000 Baht that Fred never returned would have justified me taking Joy back to my hotel.

Years passed until I got a message from Fred on WhatsApp, with a picture of him outside a shack in a Thai village. The message said,

"I'm not a two-week millionaire, this is my house."

I suppose he had no one else to tell who would understand and wanted to brag about it to someone. I asked him what he is going to do in a Thai village? Life is not easy in rural Issan especially for an overweight, 56-year-old from Liverpool. It's certainly not something I would ever dream of doing and how much had it all cost? I would imagine he has spent at least £20,000, which would include the land he would have bought from Joy's family and of course he would have been ripped off over building costs.

Things moved very fast from here! About a week later he called me from the UK. He asked me if he could come to visit me in at my house in London.

I said, "I thought you were in Thailand?"

He said, "No", that's all over now."

So, Fred came to London, he was very secretive and didn't want to say what had happened in Thailand. He just needed to get away. Eventually he told me everything, if truth be told I think he was glad to have someone to tell.

Anyway, after one of his trips to the UK, he returned to the village in Thailand to discover that the love of his life, Joy, who hadn't been blessed with the largest assets in Thailand had recently become silicone blessed. Fred asked Joy where had the money come from for the operation. She claimed her brother had paid for it.

It turned out it was an American boyfriend, one of many I'm sure who had made the silicone investment. Broken hearted, Fred had left, leaving the house he had paid for which I imagine will now be used by any of Joy's new boyfriends. Eight years of being scammed by her. He now has a broken heart and an empty wallet. I can't say I showed any sympathy, I laughed so hard I nearly had a hernia. I didn't even bother asking for my 40,000 back! Just the satisfaction of knowing that he should have listened to me on that second day in Pattaya way back then was payback. Fred went on his way to do it all again I would imagine.

I still can't quite believe that anyone could be so foolish, but they can, I had a ringside seat watching the drama all unfold. If you ever meet a guy with a Thai bar girl and he tells you that she is different, she does not like working in the bar, you know he is a no hoper and will lose everything. I hope this story wasn't too depressing but should serve as a warning to newbies heading out to the Land of Smiles.

****

Story 28.

Pla the Player

My story begins back in 2012, where I was introduced to Thailand for the first time. A friend of mine had been there before and said we should go there together on a vacation. At first, I thought,
'What am I going to do there?'
I always heard that guys go to Thailand to get girlfriends when they could not get a girlfriend at home. I didn't have any problems getting girls. I was twenty-five years old, good looking, 6'4 inches tall and 117kg of muscle. Back then I was training a lot and was a pretty good boxer at the time and was competing a lot here in Sweden. I didn't think I was going to find Thailand that amazing like most other people because of my habits with girls in Sweden, but I was wrong.

I still remember the brick wall of heat coming out of the airport in Bangkok, together with the smells and the distant talking of a foreign and unfamiliar language. I always get the same feelings when I step out of the airport, it's a fantastic feeling.

We headed off to Pattaya where one of my friends has been before. We were four friends on this trip where we arrived in Pattaya in the middle of the day and checked into our hotel around Pattaya Klang. I went to bed for a few hours due to the long trip, as I was feeling very tired.

I woke up and started wondering if I had done something dumb by coming to Thailand. We were going to stay here for fourteen days, and I was just wishing we could go back home tomorrow. We went out to eat in the evening at a seafood restaurant down by the beach. Pattaya Klang to the beach, towards Soi 7 and there it was. It was a beer bar at the same restaurant and two beautiful girls behind the bar were looking at me and smiling. I smiled back, but this was something I was used to at home as I was only twenty-five, so I did not think about it like it was a big deal.

After dinner, we went to Walking Street, strolling along Beach Road. So many girls and ladyboys grabbing at our arms trying to get us to stop and talk with them. When we got to the Beer Garden complex right before Walking Street the girls in the bars started shouting and screaming at us all competing to be the loudest. I suddenly thought, this was a great idea coming to Thailand, I like this place already.

Walking Street was a completely new and exciting experience, something I could only dream of. We had a lot of fun, drinking and partying with the girls. Later that night, I met a beautiful girl called Nim, who I had a fantastic time with and of course she ended up back at my hotel. It suddenly dawned on me why everyone loved coming to Pattaya!

For the first few days I was kind of like a dog on heat, let's just leave it at that, but eventually I met another girl I really liked called Pla. Pla was one year younger than me and we got on really well together. For the rest of my time in Pattaya I stayed with Pla until we headed back to Bangkok for two nights before heading home to Sweden. It was really difficult leaving Thailand, I felt so sad departing the Kingdom. Back home in Sweden I kept in touch with Pla through Skype almost every day for a while after our trip. But like I mentioned, I always had girls at home as well. After a few weeks I started to forget Thailand. Pla was sad because of this, I told her and was completely honest about girlfriends in Sweden.

The following year I was booked on a flight back to Thailand again. Everyone at work asked me why I was visiting Thailand again as I had been there already and recently. One of my colleagues sarcastically asked me if I was going to Pattaya for the girls? I told him and the other guys sitting around the table that I had more girls than all of you put together and your whole life revolves only here in Sweden, so no, I was not going to Thailand just for girls!

Some of my friends who have been to Thailand told me that we understand what Thailand is like as the women treat you like a God and that's exactly how I feel when in Thailand and let's face it, who would not like that feeling? I just want to say that when I am in Thailand, I am very respectful and polite to people, if people are polite to me then I return the politeness.

So back to Thailand and this second trip and this time we are staying in Thailand for three weeks. I told Pla that I was coming back, and she was happy to hear I was coming back and wanted to meet me right away. I met her and spent all my vacation with her once again. She told me the usual stuff that you so often talk about on your channel,

"She does not go with customers. She sent most of her money back to her family. No one wanted to bar fine her anyway. She was unpopular."

The usual script, but I knew none of what she was telling me was true, I just ignored it and didn't really care, it was just BS.

The BS aside, we had a fantastic time together, she took me every day to see all the local tourist attractions around Pattaya which I enjoyed. We also went to Koh Larn Island where we enjoyed some great, local food. I also took part in some Thai boxing just for fun, I beat a German guy which only added to the fun, not because he was German, but because I won the boxing match.

When it was time to leave Pattaya I was once again very sad, and Pla appeared to also be sad, but we all know that these girls can act very professionally. Anyway, Pla passed a piece of paper to me. When I read it, it had Pla's full Thai name along with her bank account number. She said,

"I don't like to work in the bar, if you can send me money every month I can stop working and wait for you to come back in my village."

I know the game as my friends had pre-warned me, so I politely told her that I did not make that much money back home so could not give her a monthly income, however, she was a really nice girl who had taken care of me for all of my holiday so on the day of my departure from Pattaya, I gave her some cash, I felt she deserved it. If I am honest with myself, I actually felt quite sad for these girls working in the bars. Although Pla and I got on well and we both had a good time, I know some foreigners treat the girls very badly and this is something I will come back to later.

Same routine, I get back to Sweden and contact Pla in Thailand by Skype but after a while I met a Swedish girl who ended up becoming my full-time girlfriend. I explained this to Pla, she was furious!

Several months after telling Pla about my Swedish girlfriend I get a message on Facebook; the message reads exactly like this:

'Hey! This is Pla's boyfriend. I have been her boyfriend for over a year. I have paid all her bills, etc. I just want to tell you that she has double played us, and a hell of a lot of other guys. It seems like she always had at least three or four boyfriends at the same time with an endless stream of defectors and newcomers coming into the picture. She sent the same love letters, the same pictures and the same bank account number to everyone. Hope you got away cheaper than me. Regards Philip.'

I texted him back and told him that I not been sending her anything. I also told him that the only thing she got from me was food, drinks and a bed to sleep in when I was there. I also told him that I gave her some money at the end of my stay, nothing else. I asked him how he got access to her messenger on Facebook? He text me back and told me,

"I helped her recover a lost password to her email. What I found was a pandora's box of betrayal. One can only be impressed by her scheming ways. Here, where I live it is called "Sun and Spring" and is punishable by law. Pla has been doing this on a large scale. It is unbelievable how she has been able to keep all the guys apart. I have talked to her for all the hours in the day and for over a year and she has also been courted by many others in the same way."

Not only was she able to manage several different boyfriends at the same time but she also found time to reel in new ones and never get found out until now. I got the odd message from Pla telling me that she misses me, but I never replied. I guess she does not know that the game is up, and I know all her dirty little secrets. They say, "Never say never," right?

Well sometime after this I broke up with my Swedish girlfriend and started replying to Pla's messages because even after I found out about her, I still liked her and just thought that I could control the game and make the best out of a bad lot if that makes sense. I am kind of old fashioned, if I am single, I play around but if I have a girlfriend, I behave myself.

I finely broke cover and asked Pla why she had lied to me? She never answered me, I guess there was nothing she could have said.

It was now 2016, I was still single and had planned another trip to Pattaya with some friends, I did not tell Pla. In Pattaya, I did a lot of partying with my friends, drinks, girls and generally running riot. One night I was lying in bed alone when I heard a lot of noise coming from the room next door. To be honest it sounded as if someone was being murdered and it went on for several minutes. In fact, it was so bad that I actually got up, got dressed and went out into the hall and stood in front of the door for a better listen. There were terrible screams coming from inside of the room! I pounded on the door, and it suddenly went quiet.

I had held my thumb over the peephole of the door so anyone inside could not see who was knocking. Suddenly the door sprang open! I couldn't believe what I was seeing! A girl was being held by three Indian guys on the bed, a fourth guy had opened the door. I can't say here what they were doing to her as it is YouTube, but needless to say, she was not a willing participant. The girl looked at me and screamed in pure desperation for help. I was furious… I pushed into the room and shouted at them to let her go! They released the girl and she fall to the floor crying. The Indian guy at the door behind me tried to hit me. I was in great shape, and I knew that four of them was no problem as I was raging. I never start fights but the guy who tried to hit me went down on the floor in around two seconds flat. The other three saw this and decided they were not going to have a go and did not move. I shouted at them, calling them everything I could think of,

218

I had never been so enraged! I almost wished the other three had started to have a go so that I could have taken them out to at least give the girl some payback. I went over to the bed, and picked up the sobbing girl in my arms, I then picked up her clothes and took her into my room. I gave her one of my T-Shirts to put on along with a towel to dry her eyes. I was trying to comfort the girl as best I could when there was a knock at my door, I thought to myself that these guys have finely worked up some courage and want to have a go at me, I was ready.

I opened my door; it was the one guy I had knocked out with two of the staff from reception. He told the staff that I had attacked him for nothing, hitting him and then I had taken the girl against her will out of their room. I told the guy to go and F himself and said he should think himself lucky I did not pulverize him. The girl by now was in the shower cleaning up, I called her and asked her to explain in Thai to the staff what had happened to her. The girl was called Apple, a very common nickname in Thailand.

Anyway, after she explained to the staff what the four guys had done to her and my role in everything, the four of them were thrown out of the hotel there and then. The story goes that one of the guys went down to Beach Road, done a deal with this girl, went back to his room where his three friends lay in wait to take full advantage of this poor girl, what could she do against four guys?

Apple stayed the night with me, but nothing happened, it was out of genuine pity for her as I truly believe she was in shock after the terror she had suffered at the hands of these four guys. The next day I asked her if she would like to join me at a restaurant, she said yes and that she felt safe and protected with me. I will be honest here, I liked Apple. It turns out that she was from Khon Kaen in Issan. We had two beautiful weeks together, before I went back to Sweden again. She thanked me for helping her and called me her Superman.

She hated the life in Pattaya, so she went home to Khon Kaen after I left. I had a nice time with both Pla and Apple back then and we are still friends. Now and then Pla texts me that she misses me and that she is building a house in her hometown with her British boyfriend, I wish him luck God knows he needs it with Pla. I hope Pla has learned her lesson and stays loyal to him. Apple moved from Pattaya back home to Khon Kaen where she still lives with her family and daughter. Apple now has a boyfriend and I feel it unlikely that he will be scammed as Apple is a much more honest person than Pla, who is a player and, in the game, to win it. I think the circumstances in which I met Apple are a good place to end this story.

The girls in Pattaya don't always meet young, handsome and charming men, sometimes they have to deal with evil men such as Apple did on that awful night. I am no white Knight, but had I not been checked into the room next door God only knows what Apple's outcome would have been. I am not a superstitious man, but I believe I was checked into that room for more than a good night's rest. I will never forget Pla and Apple, they showed me so much kindness and happiness during my brief time in Pattaya.

I thank them for showing me Thailand and sharing a part of my life when I was young and naive, I'm sincerely grateful to both of them. Today, I am thirty-five years old, have a girlfriend and she has a daughter. If I should be single again, I'm 100% sure I'm going back to the Land of Smiles.

****

Story 29.

Watch Out for Fah

I first went to Thailand in 2017 and met two friends in Pattaya. It was my first time to Pattaya, so they were showing me around all the best Soi's and bars to visit. We started our bar crawl most evenings at around 9pm and ended up going to Soi 6 or 7 I can't remember which one now. Anyway, I was 'pulled' into one of the bars by a bunch of females. As soon as we entered, the manager tried to pair us all off with girls. The women were below average in appearance and barely spoke any English, but we were so drunk that we didn't care.

A few hours later, I find myself talking to another girl and not the girl I was 'hooked up' with. This other girl spoke almost perfect English and was a stunner. I thought she was a bar girl, so I tried to make a move, but she refused my attentions and made it clear she was not interested. It turns out, she was a friend of the bar owner's son and was just there to have free drinks!

I apologised and told her it's my first time in Thailand and Pattaya and she just laughed and accepted my apology. At around one o'clock in the morning my friends and I decided to go to Walking Street. Fah, who was the girl I had apologised to, and her friend (the owner's son) and a few other ladies from the bar came with us. We went into plenty of bars along Walking Street for drinks. Fah and I were getting closer, we were dancing with each other, becoming extremely flirtatious. We even kissed a few times. I wanted to take her back to my hotel or at least carry on the night, but I had no idea if she was up for it. I didn't know if Thai girls are like that and if they were that 'easy' or if I had to work at it. I knew she was single, and she wasn't with the bar owner's son because he was gay. In the end it seemed like Fah made the decision for us because as it was getting light outside, she turned to me and said,

"When are we going back to yours?"

We all know what happened after that. We would have daily aerobics sessions, when she would come to my hotel after work (she worked as a tattoo artist). Some days we would go out to the mall or restaurants, or the cinema and I would splash out for both of us. I was earning really good money, so I didn't mind splashing out. Sometimes I would give her money to get her hair done, or get a massage, or buy a couple of bottles for us at the bars and clubs.

One day she was looking at one of my watches, it was expensive, and I had been given it as a gift from my family. Fah then told me that her birthday was coming soon, and she wanted a similar watch as a present. I thought she was just thinking out loud but then she demanded that I buy her one because I 'have a lot of money'. I just laughed and jokingly said,

"Tomorrow'.

Every time she would bring it up, I would say, "Tomorrow."

Fah's birthday was getting closer, we were shopping in the mall next to the Hilton hotel and walked past an expensive watch shop. She dragged me in and told me which watch she wanted. I showed no interest. That night, after a session of aerobics, she asked again if I was going to buy the watch for her. With a serious face, I told her no. She got upset and gave me the ultimatum of buying her the watch or she will leave.

So, I opened the door and said, "Bye."

She started crying and left immediately. I went to sleep.

The next morning, I got a barrage of texts and missed calls from Fah. She kept saying how sorry she was, and she wanted to get back together and that she misses me. I decided that I was in too deep, and I should cut it off as soon as I can. I was also a bit paranoid that she might do something extreme or foolish. So, I blocked her number and moved hotels, to Jomtien.

As I was unpacking my stuff at the new hotel in Jomtien, I realised that I was missing a bottle of expensive aftershave. I went back to the hotel I had just left and searched the room I had stayed in, but it wasn't there. I then remembered how Fah would always use my cologne, especially the missing bottle as she said it was her favourite and she wanted one. That's when I realised she took my cologne.

Anyway, to conclude the story, I stayed in Pattaya for too long. What was supposed to be a five day stay ended up being a two and a half week stay because of Fah. I didn't have long left so I decided to head back to Bangkok and finish the rest of my vacation with friends. And if you're wondering what happened to Fah?

Well, she found me on Facebook, but I didn't accept her friend request. I just blocked her.

****

PETER HOPKINS

Story 30.

Lost Control

I have a story to share with you that has
equally amused and grossed out my
friends when I've told it to them. When
travelling to and from Thailand because
of there being no direct flights from the
North East of England I normally fly to
Bangkok via Dubai with Emirates airlines
with a two-to-six-hour layover depending
on direction and which one of their flights
from Dubai to Bangkok I can get booked
on.

After a fun two weeks in Thailand in
February 2020 visiting Bangkok, Hua
Hin and then Udon Thani and some of its
surrounding cities it was time to make my
way back home. As I was travelling down
from Isaan, I booked the last Thai Smile
flight from Udon Thani at about 8pm, it's
an easy one-hour flight to Bangkok
airport, arriving a little after 9pm. With
Emirates out of BKK to Dubai there were

three flight choices 9.30pm, (which wouldn't work out with the flight coming from Udon Thani), 1.30 am (the flight I was booked on) and 2.30 am (which leaves a very tight connection time in Dubai).

After landing in Bangkok, I proceeded to head through domestic arrivals to pick up my luggage, then head to the exit and go up to fourth floor to check-in for my next flight. The Emirates check-in counters are on row T, or U I think, the opposite end to where I'd come up the escalators from domestic arrivals, so after weaving in and out of the crowds of tourists I finally made it to the row and joined the queue for check-in. The queue was quite long snaking backwards and forwards on itself several times through the cordons set up, but with lots of counters open and a couple of friendly Thai staff to guide you to the correct line and then a few more at the front prompting people to the next counter as soon as one became free (including sending people to counters reserved for 1st class, business, groups, etc...), the queue moved at a steady pace and before long I was on the last leg on the queue facing the counters.

It was while there that I noticed an older grey-haired guy come up the channel that they had set up as an exit to funnel you out towards departures once you'd finished checking in. This guy was looking to jump the queue and was making his way to the last counter once it became available. A male Thai airline staff member who was marshalling the front of the queue quickly spotted him and rushed up to explain that he'd come up the exit and he has to go back and join the queue like everyone else. The older man just stood there mumbling/slurring something but ignoring any instructions. By this point I had moved forward a little and had a better view of the man, he was in a t-shirt and a pair of white shorts, which were heavily stained yellow around the crotch area.

After a few more attempts at persuasion with the help of a female colleague, including trying to lead him by his elbow which didn't work, I assumed the airport worker must have given up for an easy life and decided to allow the old man to jump the queue and proceed to check-in on the last counter once it became available. After trying to check in with something that wasn't a passport and over hearing the two airport staff trying to get through to the slurring man (who was speaking some kind of broken drunken English, being rude and acting like the Thais were in wrong), that he needed a passport to check-in and what he handed over wasn't a passport and looked from a distance like the card holders hotels give you to keep your room keycard in, etc.. This went on for a few minutes, they eventually got him to open his bum bag and found his passport and proceeded to check him in and put his case on the scales.

It was while doing this that I noticed the two Thai's suddenly jump back slightly and because he didn't have the two Thai's blocking the view, everyone could see the man standing swaying at the counter had started to urinate there at the counter, it was flowing out the bottom of his shorts and splashing up off the floor.

Now the Thai's being polite and not wanting to draw any attention or embarrass the guy, carried on as normal until he was gone and then set about the job of cleaning up the mess. To say the people in the queue were shocked would be an understatement but there was worse to come. After he was finished at the counter and he turned to leave, we got a view of what could have possibly been the reason the Thai's let him jump the queue to begin with and to quickly get him out of the way. We now had a very clear view of the back of his white shorts, well what was once white shorts, there was very heavy brown stains and soiling all over the back of his shorts. We couldn't believe what we were seeing, and the thought was certainly running through my head, that he had checked in his hold luggage and had no hand luggage, so no possible way of changing out of them shorts and into some fresh clothes.

My next thought was, there were only two Emirates flights open, so I now had a fifty-fifty chance of being on the same flight as this smelly drunk and some unfortunate person is going to have to sit next to him for six hours to Dubai, talk about a way to ruin the end of your holiday.

Check-in proceeded as normal after that, although a little slower as the Thai's closed a few of the counters while the clean-up operation got underway and there was no slipping or being splashed with urine. Later on, after the usual check-in and departure stuff, I proceeded to the gate for boarding, and shock horror! The older man was on my flight and was still wearing those white shorts which were now looking worse than ever, was there more stains? I knew someone was going to have an unlucky and uncomfortable flight.

They started boarding by zone. I was waiting for zone B to be called and all the while hoping he would be boarding to a different zone and therefore a different section of the aircraft. They proceeded with zones D, then E, then F - thank God he boarded at this point, and I was more than happy that the zone I was the last to board. I settled into the flight and relaxed and never thought about that old man again for the rest of the flight. At Dubai there was a delay with one of the walkways, so the area of the plane I was on was the last to disembark and as I was in no particular rush with me having a two and a half hour transit I took my time, so never saw the older man getting off the plane.

After a bit of a walk around and refueling on snacks I went to the departure gates for the flight back to Newcastle, it was while waiting to get into the gate I noticed him at the opposite gate waiting for the same flight back to Manchester.

Thankfully he no longer had those shorts on and was instead wearing a pair of jogging pants. How he got them I will never know? Did he purchase them in Dubai? Did some kind stranger give him a change of clothes? Did the airline give him them and make him change so as not to upset the other passengers?

Now I know it's probably wrong of me to laugh or judge this person not knowing his circumstances or any possible medical conditions that could have contributed to the state he found himself in that day, or if it is a simple case of what most people, I've told this story to think it is - an older man having too much fun on the last day of his holiday and too much to drink. But I think there's one thing everyone can agree on, that wearing a pair of white shorts all day and then a night flight is a very bad idea unless you have a change of clothes in your hand luggage.

****

Thank you for reading and enjoying the viewers stories I have included in this book.

Please leave a review on my Amazon page if you so wish, as this will encourage more people interested in Thailand life to purchase the book.

If all goes well, there will be more books in this series, as I have hundreds more stories written by viewers of my YouTube channel, **"Thailand Bound".**

PETER HOPKINS

Manufactured by Amazon.ca
Bolton, ON